TO SOME ____ ____
PEOPLE, KEN AND MARY,
WARM AND PLEASANT
THOUGHTS.

Charlene Mihelich

VINTAGE MEMORIES

by

Edward Mihelich

Printed by:
Johnson Graphics
P.O. Box 317
Decatur, MI 49045
(616) 423-8782

ACKNOWLEDGMENTS

My apologies to many of the aged, whom I have inadvertently failed to address. Needless to say, that there are countless numbers in our city, who are walking encyclopedias, whose pages of memories will perhaps never be opened.

Words of sincere gratitude go to the many readers of my first edition, and who have encouraged me to follow through with a sequel.

Once we have ceased to make known the thoughts of our immediate family, and have forgotten our personal lineage, who will it be to continue what we have lost? I personally dread the day when I will no longer be able to record the memoirs of our senior citizens, or elaborate on the diverse cultures of our next-door neighbors and of those living abroad.

I would like to consider myself as being forever conscious of the elderly, who they are, how well they are, and how they fare in today's society. Since I myself have reached that stage in life, I enjoy the company of the aged. However, I admire the youth of today, their quick comprehension of modern technology, but their experience in life is just beginning.

PREFACE

The other day, as I looked through the patio window, I couldn't help but notice the season of autumn showing-off a spectacular and colorful display of falling leaves. It reminded me of people shedding a thousand memories, memories that lie dormant with windless days, memories that fly with sudden gusts of wind, and finally, memories that flow with a river's current, only to vanish forever.

Before the door closes on our Second Millennium, I would like to record what memories still abound in our midst. These I will find coming from the minds of the elderly, or from those whose stories possess wisdom, experience and understanding.

It is such a joy for me to watch and listen to these people, telling me about their lives as children, as adolescents, and finally, as adults. Just telling me about their life would suffice. In their conversations I would find sound bits of philosophy, that would astound me.

Being in the presence of these brave and interesting people was most rewarding for me. But what was most satisfying was that all the thoughts of my subjects would inevitable enrich the minds of all my readers. And that in time other generations would benefit by the shedding memories of falling leaves.

A most reverent salute to a
distinguished cleric, historian
and linguist, extraordinaire,

Victor Rogulj, O.F.M. CONV.

TABLE OF CONTENTS

DOROTHY STARR JORDAN

Dorothy Starr Jordan was the first person whom I interviewed in the course of my writings beginning in '92. She was then a resident of the former Gateway Plaza. Her story was inadvertently omitted in my first published collection of stories. Should she or any of her kin read this addition, please accept my apologies for this omission. At this writing I am unable to tell you whether she is living, or has reached her eternal reward. I am grateful, however, that she did leave me with some thoughts of her early home life. She left me a writing entitled, Soul to Soul, which portrayed the attributes of love, perseverance, courage, determination and gratitude. She began with:

"One morning at 10:55 some fifty-four years ago, Mrs. Louella Bruce, my dearest mother, gave birth to twins. Unfortunately, later on one of the twins passed away. My twin sister only lived for a few hours. God decided to let me live, and sometimes I wonder why? But now I know I had a normal childhood, even though we were poor, but there was so much love then. My mother raised five children and took in laundry. I came from a broken family. My dad left when I was two years old. I was the youngest of the five, one brother and four sisters. The most hurting thing in my childhood came when I was eight years old. Not knowing what hurt me made me a responsible, independent, sensitive and a caring person toward my fellow man. One day when my mother washed a lot of clothes and when she finished she asked me and my brother to take the basket of clothes walking across town. We took the

1

basket of clothes and sat on a tree stump too ashamed to pass all our friends and schoolmates. Then it began to get dark, and we decided to take the clothes. We were three hours late. When we returned home we knew we had it coming. My mother asked us where we had been. We told her the truth, because if we had lied, she might have killed us. We merely said that we were ashamed, so she quietly told us to sit down. She had a story to tell us. She began by saying you should never be ashamed of any kind of work you do, as long as it is honest. So she told us a story about her mother when she had to work as a slave, and then the tears began to flow, and then she said, "now, do you understand what life is all about and the future?" That was the worst whipping I have ever had. Still today I go through life and I hold my head up and press forward as long as I am honest. As I sit here writing, my mind dwells on the places where I lived. Alone as usual, drinking coffee I look around at all the good people who have given their lives to honest work. I see people of all cultures now retired and now feel that they are of no use to society anymore. Some are in here because of some handicap or disability like me. It is more like a home here, for love has no colors. We are all treated the same. I am sure that there are a few people who do not get along with anyone or any place. The majority of the people are wonderful who still have a lot to contribute to society. There are some very sweet and brilliant people who live here. We are not asking for miracles, but all we ask for is someone to talk to soul to soul. Recently I had a bad fall on the ice. I was so hurt and depressed. I had been doing so well, but still felt depressed. I went downstairs and everyone was sitting in the dining room. I began to cry and I could see the pain in their faces. A lady resident came up to me in a wheelchair. She could not walk for she only had one leg, but she said all you need is a little hug. She was a Caucasian lady, and this is why love has no colors. How kind of her to say that, for I needed that hug. I would give anything to my neighbor across the hall. She is my name sake (Dorothy). She is so giving of herself to everyone, and as kind, always having a joke or a poem. She is like a sister to me. You see, God has a way of putting people in the right place at the right time. There are many people in here that are kind to me. I know I can always go to them when I have a problem that is too big for me. Most of all we cannot forget the father of all of us in here, Mr. Leon Smith, our manager. I go to him, cry out to him and he always has time to listen. This is so true, he is the same with all of us. Mr. Smith deserves so much credit. His job is not easy, but he loves doing what he does being fair and honest. I also recommend the staff here especially our guard, Jerry, who watches the people going in and out. He knows every face. We never have to wait if something is broken, as it is fixed the same day, if possible. They all try to make this a home not a building. We have very special dinners on Thanksgiving. It is so beautiful with so much food. On Christmas, too, we have much food and fun. Everyone receives a gift. We were also blessed to have the honorable mayor of Niles to play Santa Claus, who also presented more gifts. Now, how blessed can we be. We were also blessed to have our supervisor give us a remarkable speech. I have lived here five years, and every holiday is very special for us. I wish first to thank God and I also wish to thank Mr. Edward Mihelich for giving us the opportunity to express our views as well as our hearts. I do pray that someone reads this and will know that Gateway Plaza is a real home and not just a building. As I said before, we are not asking for miracles, just someone to talk to, soul to soul. Please remember that love has no colors, Peace and blessing. Gratefully yours."

"I'M NOT ALONE!"

"My mother is watching me, and she's sure within eye-shot of you, too! I was born just a few days ago, and my legs are still a bit wobbly, so I'm taking a rest, and besides I don't want to let anybody know that I am here. I really wanted to hide from that mushroom hunter. I think it was my big eye and large ears that gave me away. I got pretty scared, when he started to walk towards me, but then I knew I was safe, knowing that my mother was a few trees away from me. This was going to be my mushroom patch, too!"

For the reader this is indeed the time of the year when some people are lucky to see the wonders of nature. My nephew, John Bierwagen, was one of the lucky ones. He told me that he was looking for some of those spring tasty tidbits, when he spotted a fawn lying on dried leaves. He had enough time to back track to his house and locate his camera, then returned without too much commotion to capture on film this creature of the wilds.

This photo brings back the moments that I, too, came upon a fawn resting underneath the roots of a huge ol' spruce. I was trout fishing that day, and had a feeling that I was being watched. There she stood in midstream waiting for me to make the next move. I left both to continue to enjoy the comforts of their home.

Another moment comes to mind the day a newborn ran direct into my arms as I slouched in the thick ferns. I held it momentarily as it bleated for its mother, which you knew stood somewhere nearby. Driving the highways of the Upper

4

Peninsula, I had the rare occasion of seeing a fawn and its mother during nursing time. I regret now that I do not have any proof of seeing the creatures of the forest.

At the moment I cannot believe that John still had time to go back home, located his camera and return to take a picture of this napping fawn. Could be that this newborn wanted to show the world what it looked like in a camouflaged setting.

One really never knows that while he roams the wild kingdom, he may just witness a first! We are very much aware of the wonders of mankind, but the wonders of nature are truly phenomenal.

So, the next time you're planning to hit the trail to pick those spring tidbits, or looking for that favorite bend in the river, or just absorbing the greenery, be sure that you take along that camera that you left on the living room table.

"I'm there, just let me be."

NILES' FIRST NINE-LETTER HOLDER

I find it so comforting to write about the past, and find it very discouraging when people are bored about what took place fifty years ago or so. It is rather unfortunate that some readers just don't wish to accept what already had transpired in the course of time. Why is it so difficult to admire our older leaders? I'm talking about people who have excelled in various fields, such as politics, technology, religion, sports and medicine. Why not give credit where credit is due? If you're one of those who find it so hard to give credit, at least give it a try. You're not going to believe this, but in time it will pay you dividends!

I finally found someone who deserves some recognition during his life span in the City of Niles. So, the other day I asked him to tell us something about his high school days back in the 40's. I pictured him digging in his closets, in his basement, looking in old boxes and storage places. So, what I am about to tell you came from an old musty scrap book, and believe me, did I find the goodies. I thought for a moment that he would resent the word musty, but where else do most of us find some family history? And after years of being exposed to the elements, don't expect it to have that brand new smell.

Those of you who lived in that era, will remember that the high school was located where now Uncle Sam pays his letter carriers. Now I am going to talk about all the laurels this scrappy kid was given during all those years he sat in those classrooms. Niles High School handed him awards for participating in the Band Bounce, Senior Play, Glee Club, Variety

7

Show and Octet. All this besides his books!

Without question the greatest recognition we can give this man, is that he was Niles' first nine-letter man, one letter in Cross-Country, two in football, three in basketball, and three in Track. I believe that was the makings of an all-around-athlete.

Not only did this guy like to run and jump, he loved music and sang remarkably well. He still enjoys whistling, often imitating our songbirds. After setting various records, running and jumping like a deer, shooting baskets, and tackling football opponents, he finally left the halls of Ivy in 1943.

I asked him who was responsible for helping him along the way of sports, and he said, "Joe Whitwam and Chet Davidson." The athlete became Mr. Whitwam's assistant.

It wasn't too long after graduation that our high jumper joined the Navy, and once the Naval Officer found out what he could do, he became a physical instructor throughout the Midwest and Southern Naval Training Stations. My eye was peeled on that scrap book, and read that at age twenty, he was the Southern A.A.U. heavyweight champion, and respected by many in boxing circles.

When he reached that coveted age of thirty-six, he tore up the bowling alleys with his high average and high scores and while competing in a Chicago Bowling tournament in the seventies, he rolled a 300, and returned home with a healthy monetary purse.

He became ill at an early age, but that didn't stop him from hunting rabbits and deer. During the Big Game Season his hunting buddies would often tell him, "Why don't you try the ridges at Brevort Lake?" His answer would be like no one else's, "Nah, there ain't no deer there!"

This deer slayer owned a beagle named Peanuts, and all I can say is that this dog was a rabbit maniac. The dog's owner let me use him for one year, but that's another story!

8

I believe that I have covered all that there is to know about this athlete, bowler, boxer, family man, outdoor sportsman, and Navy Physical Instructor. Now it's time to tell you who this man is.

His name is Hank Miswick, and it just so happens that he's my brother-in-law.

TED GUSTAFSON, BREVORT'S PIONEER

After you have crossed the five mile span on Mackinac Bridge traveling north, you will enter the region known as the Upper Peninsula of Michigan. In so doing you will have seen two of our Great Lakes, namely, Michigan on your left, and Huron on your right. Your destination now is to travel West on U.S. #2. Driving along Lake Michigan for some twenty miles, you will arrive at the town of Brevort. I would like that you and your company to stop and meet an elderly man, that will tell you a story about his life in this territory. Listen now to the many words of Ted Gustafson.

Ted is an offspring of Swedish parents, who were immigrants from Geta Oland, Sweden, which is now part of Finland. Ted's parents settled in this part of North America for obvious reasons. Living along the North Atlantic, fishing became their livelihood, and so the shores of Lake Michigan, especially at Brevort location, was their first and only stop.

Fishing this new body of water was quite an experience, as their daily catch would now be fresh water fish. I was told that fishing was exceptionally good in the early 1900's. Ted told me so many things, so did his immediate family. I marveled at the way he said things. His gestures told me even more, especially when he described about the time when his parents built a fourteen-room house to accommodate the growing family. At one time there were ten people occupying this building. There were five boys, the oldest of whom was Gunner, followed by Reuben, Elmer, Ted and Alvin. They had three sisters, namely, Edith, Rose and Esther. Today the sole survivor of these incredible Swedes is Ted, with whom I became acquainted in the early 50's.

In due time most of these Scandinavians became commercial fishermen. At one time I had the good fortune of accompanying Ted on one of his daily runs. Believe me, this was quite an experience, especially watching him pulling in his net with a healthy catch of whitefish. Some of the fish had sea lampreys attached on to them, while others had the markings of once being attacked by these predators. There was a time when they became an uncontrollable menace in the Great Lakes. The State Fisheries stepped in and helped somewhat, but in recent times I was told that they are beginning to lurk the deep waters.

During my lengthy visit with this man of nature, he spoke of the fishing sites of the early Indians. Driving along Lake Michigan some years ago, there were tamarack pilings that were clearly visible in the water which were used for setting fishing pond nets. It didn't take too long for the white man to copy the ways of the American Indian.

As he spoke, he brought about the incidents that occurred during his adventurous lifetime. You, the reader, will note that I called these people the incredible Swedes. But it was what they did, and how they did it so extraordinarily. To begin with, Ted's father caught a sturgeon that hit the scale at two hundred ninety-seven pounds. He mentioned that the Indians were primarily after this gigantic fish. He continued with the time that he himself landed a musky with a two pound rainbow in its mouth. His fishing stories were many, and I wished that I had accompanied him on every expedition. Of course, we talked about smelting season, which to this day, lures scores of dippers for the spring's catch.

Each time the fishing was poor, Ted would say, "there would be times that the going was good, and times when the times were bad." I liked the way he said that! He worked with

11

lumber when the "going was bad", and I believe this was the time when he built a cabin for hunters that came from other parts of our State or neighboring States. He ended up with building twelve units, thus accommodating thirty hunters. He and his lovely wife Ethlyn named their establishment the Blue Horizon.

Ted had that look on his face as though he could tell me his whole life in one breath. Believe me, there are not too many men around, especially at his age, that would be able to remember so many things, so many detailed things. Now he's beginning to tell me about the time he nailed a beautiful buck off Worth's Road. You might have guessed that he has that outstanding mount in his living room, where else?

More fishing on deck! There were days on end, that he and his brothers would be out at least four miles on the Frozen Lake fishing for some Mackinac Trout. He recalls the day that he landed a forty-seven pound trout with a lawyer fish in its mouth. Spearing was their game, and after they braved the wind, the snow and cold, they returned home with a catch that they talked about for a half a century!

Let's stay on land for a moment. Somewhere on the CCC roads he's in search of squirrels and partridges, and while he's out there, he sighted a black bear carrying a bunch of leaves for its winter den. He didn't hesitate to tell me that he bagged this beast. He told me about the time that his brother killed a cub, and he almost paid for it with his life, as the mother charged him. Some DNR people have been known to tell us that black bears are harmless. I must tell you that I totally disagree, as I had a terrible experience when I was a teen in the Copper Country. Ted goes on to say that one year he saw five bears feeding on beechnuts, which was an unusual sight to see that many huddled together.

This ninety-one year old Swede really hasn't let any grass grow under his feet. His daughters tell me that he was able to

12

tell us where all the windfalls lay, the places to find the most deer, the places where the best mushroom patches were, and all the partridge havens, the beaver ponds that teem with scrappy brook trout. I'm sure he knows all the bends of the rivers in Mackinac County.

In the course of our conversation we talked about his early education. He was schooled in Brevort, and after finishing high school, he spent some time at Ferris State where he studied some business courses. He is well versed in so many things. They tell me that he enjoys reading. His hobbies today are gardening, even though early frosts threaten his harvest. During our last visit with him, I noticed a contraption that he engineered to water his garden. I imagine in the span of life, he has engineered countless other projects.

The Gustafsons have reared five children, the eldest of whom is Deanna, now a Canadian Citizen, followed by Phyllis, now living in St. Ignace, then Nancy, a resident of Kalamazoo, followed by Richard, residing at Brevort, and finally Beatrice a resident of Painesville, Ohio. From this clan there are five grandchildren, that one day will reminisce about the activities of their grandparents, uncles and aunts. I am sure that they will talk about their foreign Swedish and French heritage.

The name of Brevort has as its original name spelled as Brevoort. Ted's daughter, Deanna, sent me a lengthy and elaborate research on the history of Brevort, which explains why there are two spellings. This writing is a story in itself. The present populace of this community has accepted the name of Brevort. In recording the memoirs of this region, it is, as I see it, Little Sweden, with a smacking of French and other European lingoes.

I believe it was sometime in August 1997, that I wrote to Ted's four daughters asking them to record some thoughts about their dad, as they were growing up along the shores of

Lake Michigan. All four girls came through with flying colors. At the moment I am still waiting for word from their brother, and this will complete the picture of this Swedish offspring. Believe me, it's quite a picture!

Behind this pioneering Swede, there stands an equally great woman. This was emphatically stated by Phyllis, and I considered this to be a bit of sound philosophy. This family said so many nice things about their father. They wanted to tell me and so many others, that he was always aware of where his family was and what it was doing.

He personally told me about his partridge hunts, but I didn't know that the eyes of his daughter were used as spotters! The way he talked and gestured, the forest was his life. Of course, Carl Worth's place became a rendezvous for those who enjoyed the outdoors—who got what? how many, etc. What memories one can relate whoever tramped the trails with this fisherman. There's no doubt that his clothing was always saturated with the smell of the wilds.

I marveled at this man's Sunday attendance at Church, which was just a stone's throw from his house. The girls tell me that if he was lax about his faith, one of his sisters who also lived in the neighborhood, saw to it, that he, too, would be counted in the congregation. As time went on, he became a pillar of his Lutheran Church.

Now let's go down again to one of the fishing piers, where Ted and his brothers, a few other Gustafsons, followed by the Mavelsons and Halbergs. So you see, a close bunch of Swedes, who talked about fishing when the sun rose and set. They talked about their boats, their nets, floats and leads, and, of course, always learning to read the signs of nature. Their setting out to the sea was on most occasions worry free, but their return trips were at times of utmost concern. Once the fleet came in, there was fish to clean, to pack and to ship. I picture the Gustafson children tearing down the beach when they first learned about the boats' landing. They never talked about eating too much fish, but they always talked about their wonderful experience, and how good it was to be a native of Brevort, and how rewarding it was to be reared by such loving parents.

It seems that his sister, Edith, became a nemesis whenever something of a Scandinavian concern was involved. If the affair was illegal or illicit, there weren't any questions asked, why?

As I record all these thoughts, I picture a certain closeness to each other and to the general public. As years passed, there were so many people that had stopped to say "hello", to ask for directions, or just to chat over a cup of coffee, which spells perfect congeniality.

I may sound repetitious, when I keep telling you about fishing, especially combing the shores at Brevort, where the Carol Dee used to dock, and all the happy memories that were associated with it.

There were articles in the girls' stories that certainly brought back some fond memories, when I was growing up, such as picking berries for my mother to preserve for the winter months. These are just pieces of outstanding memories that we can cherish and retain for years to come. It's amazing how some children picked out the names of some of their father's working horses.

Being that I was once a frequent visitor in these parts, and enjoyed the wilds, I would stop by Ted Gustafson's place for directions to a trout stream or Epoufette's ice fishing Bonanza. There's no doubt that he taught me the tricks of this trade, and finding the rubs and scrapes of the white tail. I became obsessed with trout fishing ever since I was a kid, and there is no doubt in my mind that this man helped to enkindle this obsession. Just the thought of wilderness does something to my soul. There are scores of things that come to mind, speckled trout making the top of the list, followed by partridge hunting, snowshoe rabbits and rabbit stew, hunting deer on the Brevort Trail, and thinking of venison roasts. What other exciting adventure is there left, and what other delectable fish is there, besides the taste of Lake Michigan trout and whitefish?

Deanna, our Canadian neighbor, tells about her father watching the sunrise in the morning and sunset at night, reminded those who were to embark on seagoing vessels, "red sky at night, a sailor's delight, and a red sky in the morning was a sailor's warning".

I must tell you that I enjoy eating fish, but when I go to a restaurant, I do not order any, even though the menu may tell me "the catch of the day", that I can get at Gustafsons! When Beatrice wrote about her dad's fish, whether baked, boiled, broiled or smoked, my mouth watered.

As I mentioned earlier in the narrative, that the daughters of this Scandinavian did a remarkable research on this man whom they called Daddy. They took such great delight in telling us that they had such a good and happy life. They enjoyed talking about the good ol' days, helping their dad, their mother in whatever work there was to do.

When all the Swedes have run their course in life in this small and memorable fishing town, who will continue to decorate and raise the Swedish Mid-summer Pole? It would be most regrettable that this rich culture pass away.

Writing about Ted Gustafson, his work, his pleasure, his religious affiliations, and his family was indeed an honor. May I extend my gratitude to all who have submitted their written accounts of their beloved Daddy.

Now lets cross over a few well-trodden paths and visit some of Ted's fellow-countrymen. We do know that all were expert tillers of the soil, and truly the tenders of their fishing nets.

You might say that this little colony was also Little Scandinavia. The folks that usually had the first news from their homeland were Mr. & Mrs. Axel Mavalson, the latter of which was the local Postmistress. In this ethnic group were the Carlsons, Matsons, Holmbergs, Vogts, Hallbergs and Sundquits. In due time I became acquainted with all these immigrants and their offspring.

Since my brother-in-law, Ted Miswick, preceded my arrival to this territory, he introduced me to a Swede, named Harley Hagen, who knew every aspect of the Call of the Wild. He and Ted both had unmatched identical hunting strides, ones characterized by long and vigorous steps. Following them down the Ol' Mackinac Trail was truly a sight.

There were latecomers to this coveted place along West U.S. #2. Owen and Barbara Jorgensen not only brought with them their Danish Culture, but they were both blessed with musical and artistic talents.

This concludes my brief and personal account of the neighboring folks that made up this town of happy people.

Home base for the Gustafson Fishery

A Remarkable Family Tie

THOSE INCREDIBLE SWEDES

A few years ago I met an ol' Swede, whose parents were some of America's early immigrants. I was very fortunate to have captured his treasured memories. He told me about his work on the railroad, about the times he shoveled coal for the engine, the many times he sounded the train's whistle in the wee hours of the morning as it sped through some tiny town. He was very sad when he told me about people losing their lives at railroad crossings. I speak here of Charles Hedstrom, one of Niles' railroad pioneers. He was only ninety-eight when he finished his race in life.

I heard of another Swede, who used to farm around Anderson Road in Cass County. Russell Ellsworth Anderson told me that he was eighty-six years and five months old. He made sure that he added those extra months, not to make him look older, but to complete the 20th Century, and then some.

His grandparents came to this country back in 1873. He was so proud to tell me about his bloodline, and believe me, he's trying so hard to reach that pinnacle of old age—yes, he's looking forward to it! This kind of puts many of us to shame, when we're trying so desperately with our new technology to give us that youthful appearance, you know, that face lift. I wonder how many of us at his age would continue to drive golf balls at Hampshires fairways, and throw strikes at White's Lanes. He obviously doesn't have time to think about getting old. Yes, he even has a license to drive. He enjoys his life and his life-style.

He and his wife, Florence, brought three children into this

world, Mary, the first born, then another daughter, Jane, and James, who also became the tiller of the soil. Russell's father started the farm, and it was he, who at one time, worked on the Airline Railroad that ran adjacent to their spread.

While I was listening to him in the living room, he told me a little about his childhood. He always cherished the thought of going into Niles riding with his parents, with horse and buggy, of course. He said the trip took about two hours. When they'd get to town, he marveled at the tie-shed, where other farmers would meet. He would be as thrilled when his father and mother took him to the local restaurant. While in town they would give eggs and butter in exchange for flour and sugar.

The colony of Andersons lived on Anderson Rd., stretching from Pokagon Highway to U.S. #12, over hill and dale. This is when the storyteller would tell me about the many times that the horses and sleighs were often bogged down in huge snow drifts.

With his familiar drawl he continued to gesture, especially when the clan got together for Thanksgiving and Christmas. I told him, "May this joyous meeting continue to be!"

Russell Anderson was well versed in the education of the youth of Cass County. Naturally, he had to tell me about the time that he attended the one-room schoolhouse, named, Dibble Dale, which, by the way, still stands as a living memento of years past. He recalls the time when he attended Cass High that he substituted for a teacher who was absent. During his high school days he played on the Varsity Football Team. He graduated from Cass High in 1929.

Back on the farm he worked with his two brothers, Milo and Oliver. Russell was quite saddened when Milo died because of a farming accident. After much work on the farm, he was still involved with school politics, first on Dibble Dale School Board, and also on the Cass County School Board.

While serving as president of the Cass Public Schools, he had the distinct honor of giving his children their graduation diplomas. Even with all these school boards, he managed to be on the Board of the Farmers' Market. And when his work on the various boards was completed, he and his wife Florence would tour the World. Even after he lost his lovely companion, he continued his adventurous journeys. Little wonder then, why he knew so much about this complex universe.

On the Anderson's vast acreage the family harbored dairy cattle, grew corn, potatoes, soybeans, and a plant that produced peppermint oil.

Russell was indeed a man of diverse interests. I asked him, "Mr. Anderson, what do you miss most in your life-time?" He smiled and said, "See that barn out there? We built that in '29, and I miss the smell of that building, the hay and the animals, and I must say that I miss the smell of the farm."

As we were walking into the kitchen, this Swede was happy to tell me that he and his brother Oliver built this house. He showed me a couple of things that required a lot of skill and hard work. All their lumber was sawed and planed by these two builders. You can't imagine the pride that the owner of this ol' house has, when all the Andersons get together!

Just as I was leaving, he handed me a written tribute about a lovely lady, his very dearest friend and wife, Florence. Here are a few excerpts of that personal message: "She was a sports-minded person, but she always had time for the sick and injured. . . .she loved the Lord, attended Church regularly, taught Sunday School classes and sang in the choir. We should be glad that we lived at the time and in the place, so as to be touched by her life."

From what I, the writer have observed, this well-traveled man has led a good and satisfying life, and has certainly paved a way for all those to follow him.

WORDS OF ROMAN STATESMAN
FITTING TODAY

I have read and translated the works of an ancient author for some time now, and I thought that it's high time that others meet this man. His name is Marcus Tullius Cicero, A Roman Statesman, an orator and a prolific writer. He was in all probability the pioneer of Roman Classical Literature.

Students mastering the study of Latin will tell us that translating Cicero's writings is indeed time consuming and requires much serious thought. But once the novice has conquered Cicero's style, he will discover a wealth of philosophical truths.

This Latin scholar wrote two masterful compositions, one on Friendship, and the other on Old Age, whose translations read De Amicitia and De Senectute. Perhaps a closer look at these two words allows one to find their English derivations. I, personally, find it most appropriate to discuss these qualities of a person, as they both are making headlines in our daily living.

During my years in the classroom and hallways, I would spend many hours looking at our youth and wondering how trying it must have been for an adolescent, not only to find a friend, but also to hold on to one. All of us, for that matter, wish to know what friendship really is, what it means to have a good friend and what it means to be a good friend.

According to our statesman of antiquity, friendship can only exist between the good, whose actions and lives leave no question concerning their character, and who are free from greed, lust and violence. I especially enjoyed his thought when he said that a true friend is seen as a second half, so that where his friend is, he is, and if he be rich, he is not poor, and if he is weak, his friend's strength is his, much like our proverbial usage, "a friend in need is a friend indeed."

Among this orator's fellow countrymen, friendship comprised fidelity, firm mindedness and integrity. He finally points out that the rule for this characteristic is that one should neither ask for nor consent to what is wrong.

Cicero's other writing deals with old age, which happens to be our greatest nemesis, and which all walks of life must face. All of his discourses are powerful and thought provoking, and it's very likely that our readers may not be fully aware of these bits of wisdom.

I really never thought that this time in my life would be a gift, as the author claims it is. We try so desperately at times to conceal this revered gift, but in the final analysis, it begins to show. He goes on to say, that if all ages of man are burdensome, surely he has to face the last one, which is he biggest hurdle. But Marcus Tullius does sound more consoling, when he says that if we are happy in our younger life, then we, without a doubt, will be happy at the end of our race. In his conversation with his peers, they all look forward to becoming old men. When was the last time you heard anyone say that?

True, old age does take us away from active employment, it enfeebles the body, deprives us of many physical pleasures, and it is the next step to death. But, he does leave us with this thought that the old are in better position than the young, for the one wishes to live long, and the other has already lived long.

Though He Is Ancient, His Influence on Language is Unsurpassable.

KILLER BLIZZARD '78

It all began on the eve of January 26. The skies were overcast, mild winter temperatures, and at midday snowflakes like oversized cornflakes fell gently and aimlessly. They were not persistent, but they were trying to tell us something. Maybe it was just another way of manifesting their beauty, or an indication of what tomorrow may bring. Some people were optimistically heard to say, that in spite of adverse weather forecasts, it was truly a mild wintry day. Others pessimistically predicted heavy snows.

At daybreak on Thursday, January 26, 1978, the landscape was changed. It had been viciously attacked, and it was unrecognizable and hostile. This date was to be recorded in the annals of the Midwest as having the greatest blizzard of the century. The land appeared as having no sky, and that every cloud touched the earth unloading its paralyzing cargo. The northwest winds pounded relentlessly and mercilessly, whipping and drifting snow as though it was a terrible scourge. Nothing moved and all living things just peeked to behold the devastating wonders of nature. What was once a busy thoroughfare became a pioneer wagon trail abruptly coming to a dead end. What was once a street saw no life. What was once a rural route became mountainous snowdrifts. There may have been one window in every home used as a telescope viewing a faint outline of a neighbor's house.

The news media told us and showed what was really happening outdoors. What took place in southwestern Michigan, also occurred in our neighboring States. These parts were being stalked by a killer blizzard looking for its victims. What we witnessed were stranded cars, canceled air flights, exhausted passengers at all terminals. We observed people being tossed like litter by gale force winds, travelers shoveling for their barricaded autos, snowmobiles on emergency missions. We saw municipal and county buildings stilled by a crippler. We heard city officials proclaiming their domains as disaster areas, law enforcing agencies pleading with the public to stay home and not hinder snowplows or emergency vehicles.

There were many stories passed on to local radio stations, many humorous, some tragic. People telling about their dogs howling during the night standing like wolves on huge snowdrifts, unable to reach their houses. One told about a house guest who walked to the grocery store, but whose heart was too weak to fight the storm. Another told about Good Samaritans preparing lunches for tired highway crews and marooned travelers. There was news about people saddling their horses to deliver food to the needy. Perhaps the most tragic story was the incident when an infant had died in her mother's arms while she struggled through wind and snow and frantically tried to open her door. We heard that many were without power and heat. There were other truths, I'm sure, that people wished to tell and some day will be unfolded. Whether marked in diaries, calendars, journals, memos, or on basement walls, it will be a grim reminder that a killer blizzard lurked these parts in early '78.

Schools were closed, and as one announcer put it, they were "wiped out", "shut tight", "solid shut" or just plain "forget it". The doors of education were untouched for seven consecutive days.

This part of the world shoveled, dug, pushed and climbed its way out of the ravages of a winter's scourge, somewhat like the ravages of war, where only outlines remain. At this writing it is not known how many fell victims to this stalk. The statistics could be staggering.

The front yard looked like the landscape of Mound Builders, but I managed to start the family's cars, just making believe we were going somewhere.

One of the oddities of natureùa local housewife opening the back door to let her dog out, and at that same instant a half dozen chickadees skipped in for a short stay.

The fuel supply at our home was exhausted, which prompted my snow shoeing next door for five gallons of fuel oil. Visiting my neighbor, a senior citizen, is like going to graduate school gaining wisdom. There is no book that could match his experience. Knowing that a small amount of fuel wouldn't suffice and withstand our present blast, we finally succeeded in obtaining an additional twenty gallons. This was transported from a main route, where the local distributor was met. An improvised toboggan was designed by another ingenious neighbor to carry our precious load. Together with my son and friend we walked, snow shoed and lumbered our way to our chilled house.

The storm had subsided, but there was evidence of a killer on the loose. The snows continued but the gusty winds were spent. Was it certain that this was the end of a nightmare, or was it just a resting period for another onslaught? This blizzard was ruthless and had no remorse. There was talk that another one would rip through this land.

A crew of volunteer snowmobilers just stopped in with a sled of groceries that had been ordered for ourselves and the neighbors. We chatted a while, and they told us about their battle with the wind and visibility. They traveled the entire day and even at night to help those in need of supplies. Their faces expressed much satisfaction, even the face of one who was sixty seven. Truly an example of stamina and courage.
A helicopter flew by in the night undoubtedly on a mission of mercy. There were other such flights that had helped people whose lives had been endangered by heavy snows.

"What's open down town?", one would ask, and the answer came as, "I didn't see anybody, so I really don't know." This is the third day of continuous snow, and many roads still impassable. The metropolitan areas were now just beginning to show signs of one way passage. The telephone lines were swamped with the usual questions as, "Is your road plowed?" "How are things at your house?" It was an opportune moment to find a true friend.

Radios continued to warn the public about snow accumulations and travelers' advisories, and that those traveling, do so at their own risk. Telephone conversations gave us countless stories, as one told about a man playing cards at his neighbor's for several hours during the heat of the storm, only to find that all of the house's exits were blocked when it was time for him to leave. A window was used for his escape. You would often hear about boys delivering cakes and soups to people in the neighborhood, and then returning with a happy feeling of extraordinary accomplishment.

Some family members were just now getting acquainted with each other. Perhaps it was a time when the values of life were first being unfolded. There were boxed-games that were now being played, games that had been stored and covered with dust. In many cases there were improvised amusements, and with all this togetherness, one not only found flaring tempers, but also laughter, a family medicine.

Of course, mail deliveries in rural areas have long been overdue, creating moments of anxiety for news from relatives and friends, and also putting doubts in the minds of most creditors. When Uncle Sam's Carriers would venture forth, was anyone's guess. First there had to be the glorious arrival of a monstrous snowplow to pave.the way, then and only then would others dare to follow.

They said that all grocery stores became Klondikes, and that most shelves had been emptied in a matter of hours. In some instances it was impossible to purchase milk, as farmers were unable to deliver raw milk to local producers, and for this reason hundreds of gallons were uselessly disposed of.

During our confinement we had a visitor, pleasant, courageous, though a bit exhausted by his snowshoe trek delivering groceries. One may have wondered how well he fared on snowshoes, as he traveled five hectic miles. It was an art that he had mastered while he attended Northern Michigan University. He did gave us the latest report about our city, very simply described as a very lonesome and desolate place.

We were now in the fifth day of isolation, though delighted to welcome sunny skies. Highway travel was still somewhat curtailed. A day to be remembered when some residents on Stafford Road received an ample supply of fuel oil.

The city of Niles and the adjacent territories were spared from the Russian flu epidemic, which menaced the college campuses of the Western States.

So much has transpired during these unforgettable and notable days, when moments became agonizing, acts came to be heroic and some selfish, when there were even times of looting. Bonds of friendship and family life were truly strengthened and united. The blizzard of '78 has left an indelible mark on all Midwesterners.

The people of the East Coast heard about our misfortune, but they, too, were troubled and tormented by a winter blast that struck a week later. Not only the snows, but also the winds off the Atlantic seaboard threatened all New Englanders, Bostonians and New Yorkers, who undoubtedly have recorded journals of their blizzard of '78.

Across the Continent came news that heavy rains caused landslides of mud, floods and swollen rivers in southern California. It appeared that people everywhere were being pushed by some devastating, unpredictable and uncontrollable force, which technology has so desperately tried to prevent. It is most certain that had William Shakespeare lived during America's recent adventure, he would have penned as he had so prolifically done in Early England, "Lord, what fools these mortals be!"

THE MANY FACES OF MAN

People are people, whether they live in an old castle, in a picturesque mansion, in a luxurious ranch home, in a comfortable bungalow, in a run-down shack, or in a cold, plain cardboard box. They could be from a foreign land, or they could be from the good U.S. of A., right here on my side of the tracks, or from your side.

The people I chose to write about today are you. I don't know whether you feel the same way about people as I do, but there are so many of us that hate each other in very trivial things. It could be that the limb of your tree extends a bit into your neighbor's property. Then we have the old folks who are pushed around by the young. What is really sad, is when you see this in family circles. Visit a nursing home and you'll know what I am talking about.

I hope you don't mind my talking about the many faces that I see around our community. We see so many of these in the course of our daily living, and believe me, in the last few months, there have been many sad looking faces, no jobs, not much money to go around, and some of the things that you hear from embittered people are not too pleasant.

Those of us who have lived during the Big One, the Depression, that is, you know that it was a real one, and thank goodness that we were not plagued by so many killing diseases as we have today. In spite of this very sad era, people were not known to hate as they do in these days.

For the past two years or so, I have been telling you about all kinds of faces, not only those of Michigan, but also those of other parts of this Great Land. We talked about loggers, miners, a miser, hermit, a barber, some foreigners, farmers, doctors, teachers, outdoorsmen, lawyers, pharmacists, missionaries, animals, camping, and of course, the U.P., and there are more people, places and things on the way.

Those of us who are children of immigrant parents, were told about their trip across the Atlantic Ocean. No doubt about it, many of them were your relatives, and those faces could have been German, Polish, French, Hungarian, Scandinavian, Croatian, Slovenian and the English. As we grew older, we began to realize how important this journey to the New World was for our parents. When you were in school, you studied about the immigrants, you even saw their pictures in history books, you noticed that expression on their faces. When I page through one of those books, I still look for somebody that resembles my parents. They did tell me, though, as they told you about that long trip from their native country. Everyone on the ship was told what to expect, as the steamer neared the shores of America. Do you remember when they told you about the Statue of Liberty? They all saw that torch in her hand, and thought it to be a welcome gesture, or maybe they felt that it was a light showing them what was to be seen beyond the city of New York.

But before these early settlers made their last stop, there were legal matters to take care of. The ship docked at Ellis Island, the place that most passengers resented, for the simple reason that each person had to be medically checked over by the U.S. Customs Officials. For most it was a passing grade, but for a certain few, it was a return passage to their homeland. No doubt many tears were shed, as many families were separated.

Every time I see a picture of the interior of the building on the Island, I have thoughts of my parents and relatives being led into stalls for their personal examinations. It was rather humiliating, but it had to be done. On second thought, for some it really didn't matter, for the land of fortune and prosperity were just minutes away.

There was a sixteen year old Italian boy on one of those immigrant ships. He came to this Big World all by himself. His name was Anthony Saratore. I was glad that I talked to his daughter, Marie. I can picture him telling her all about that rough trip, about the Statue of Liberty and those stalls. This goes back to the early 1900's. Marie wanted to see those planks her father once walked, so she had the good fortune of visiting the famous Ellis Island, which today is a great tourist attraction.

Our true-blue Scotsman, Andy Mollison, also brushed shoulders with those Customs Officials back in 1924. Just imagine, that's sixty-eight years ago, and he is still good timber for a conversationalist.

Once these weary and confused travelers touched terra firma, they now looked for train depots. It was at these points that the immigrants bought tickets for their railroad fare to various parts of our country. Most Slovaks chose Pennsylvania, the Poles made Michigan and Illinois their destination. The Scandinavians selected Northern Michigan and Minnesota, the States that most resembled their native land. The people from Cornwall, England wanted to be near the mining fields of Michigan and Minnesota, as did most of the other Slavic tribes. Most Germans settled in Wisconsin, and the French enjoyed the confines of Quebec, Canada, though many made their home in America.

Picture yourself as being an offspring of one of these pioneers, who took part in putting together our great nation.

BALTIC, MICHIGAN, THE HOME OF BERRIEN
COUNTY'S REGISTRAR OF DEEDS

Last week I told you that today's episode would be about Baltic, but we didn't tell you who, what or anything about this name. It just so happens that this is the birthplace of Bernice Tretheway, our County's Registrar of Deeds. Baltic is a tiny village sandwiched somewhere between some other villages named Trimountain, South Range, Painesdale and Atlantic Mine. All these places are familiar to me as my Godparents lived in Dodgeville, another hamlet, or like a relative to all the other little towns. Since I knew a few of the natives in that area, I must tell you that I had my first sauna bath in South Range, and Allie Rugani saw to it that this was to be!

Bernice sent me a little history about this territory, and I would like to share it with you. This is Copper Range Country and this is precisely why this part of the U.P. is called the Copper Country. It seems that in no matter what other part of the country I may be, as soon as I hear the word "Copper Country" mentioned, my ears become like a snowshoe rabbit!

This piece of rich copper extends from Ontonagon County through the Copper Range and on to the tip of Keweenaw County. Even the smell of the land will tell you that there's copper in the belly of this earth.

For those of you who are unfamiliar with this piece of Real Estate, all these small towns are located 'uphill' on Michigan Highway 26, some ten miles southwest of Houghton, the home of Michigan Tech, and its twin city Hancock, the site of Soumi College.

All the communities grew around the copper mines with the exception of South Range, which developed more commercially to serve other towns. The Copper Range Mining Co. owned most of the land and buildings in that area, where its people rented the houses. In the early days of mining, which would take us back to the 20's and 30's, each town would have a General Store, a Post Office, and a grade school. Entering these stores would be similar to our going to the local K-Mart, where you would find most anything to buy, and certainly a place where you would see strange faces and physiques that would stagger one's imagination. I recall seeing one such general store in a small town south of Marquette one year, and some of the people that shopped there would make ideal characters for another story.

The schools at the Range were large two-story buildings housing eight grades. They were built in this fashion to conserve heat. Like most schools in that part of the U.P., they had large yards, where the kids played and where the dogs, cows and horses roamed. Bernice tells us that she had the deepest respect for all the cows in the playground and elsewhere.

There was one high school that served all the towns, and this was located at Painesdale. School started at 8 a.m. with half-hour for lunch and dismissal at 3:30 p.m. That school is still there today and very much the pride of the young as well as the old. Back then the school train picked up students for the high school. Many of the kids walked quite a distance to catch the train. "We had quite a hill to climb to the school building," she writes. Painesdale High School was one of the few schools that had a swimming pool and tennis courts.

These were the towns where many of our early immigrants settled, such as the English from Cornwall, England, the Scandinavians, the Germans, French, the Finns, Irish and the Slavs. The mines provided them with work, and this is why they came to the New World.

The Mining Co. provided many services, some of which was the water supply, cleaning the alleys and fixing the rented houses. Each town had a clinic, and the general hospital was located in Trimountain, where the Company furnished a doctor. "In my home town of Baltic, there were three churches, the Finnish, Catholic and Methodist," she wrote. Bernice also stated that every small town had many churches and were well attended by the many nationalities.

Places of recreation were all subsidized by the Mining Co. The young had ample opportunity to participate in sports, such as baseball, hockey, ice skating and tobogganing. I personally remember the town of Painesdale as having a superb hockey team.

There was much rock in the area, as the miners would bring up rock from the various levels of the mine. I am sure that there are many rock piles that are still visible, and serve as reminders of yesteryear's productivity. Bernice wrote about the many things that are used in a mine, such as, the mining shaft, mining level, the cage or the skip, the powder room (used for blasting), the boiler house, the carbide lamp, the lunch bucket, the mine office, the machine shop, the gondolas used to ship the copper by rail.

Our informant concludes her adventurous account by telling us that all the towns still exist, but the mines are closed because of the high cost of extracting the ore. When the Company left, the people bought the houses that they had rented. The purchase price was well below the thousand mark. I am sure that many people in our cities, which include those in Berrien County, wonder what the natives do for a living in that part of Michigan, now that mining has been exhausted. Many are employed in the communities of Houghton and Hancock. There are still dense forests that surround the vil-lages, where families enjoy the flavors of wild berries and pick wild flowers for their dining room tables. For those that enjoy hunting and fishing, where else would one in the Midwest care to relax? Baltic is in that circle.

WALTON CREEK IN 1922

Back in 1922 the Interurban used to whiz by along Walton Creek headed for St. Joseph. Its starting point was South Bend, and at times there were passengers boarding the train around the Walton Road area.

The Raymond G. Mell family lived along these tracks. Today I had the occasion to visit with one of his daughters, Cleo Beckwith, by name, and she told me some nice things about the Mell farm. On their spread they had some fruit, mostly cherries. She remembers picking wild grapes, and on this one day she spotted some snakes basking in the sun, and since then the serpents have been taboo in her vocabulary. Besides the fruit, her father had a large garden. There were cows, of course, horses, chickens, and she remembers distinctly that they had seventy-five ducks swimming and diving for goodies in Walton Creek. This kind of reminds me of my niece's and her friend's farm, where they have honking geese, peeping goslings and turkeys, cackling hens, crowing Polish roosters, and a baby billygoat, named Jellybean, who, by the way, likes to eat rose bushes. They also have barking dogs! You talk about down on the farm!

I asked Cleo about school back then, and she told me that they used to attend Matchett Peak School. I wonder how many of our readers remember traveling on a steep hill called Matchett Peak? I wonder myself how many travelers were stranded on that piece of road on a stormy night in winter?

Cleo's father worked at the Kawneer Plant besides tending to his sixty some acres. I was told that the Mells were expert

38

do-it-yourselfers! She was pretty proud to tell me that they were a closely-knit family with much love and togetherness. Would that we could once again possess this rare attribute. "I remember riding with my father on a sleigh near the French Paper Mill," she said. "He always gave us undivided attention," she continued. She went on to say that her dad had a bicycle which he cherished very much, up until he bought a used Model T Ford! She laughed when she told me about the time her dad slaughtered a calf and tied the veal over the hood of the car, and while he drove it to a friend's house something happened. Being that the roads were muddy and rutty, the T flipped over on its side and so did her father and his veal! "It was a mess," she said, "and so was he."

Cleo is a soft-spoken person, but I'll tell you one thing, her stories are endless! They used to have a booth at the Farmers' Market where their produce was hauled in from their big garden. Since they had quite a cherry orchard, they would annually preserve hundreds of jars of cherries, all supposedly sealed tight. Some time late in the fall they noticed that many, many jars had spoiled, the contents of which they gave to the chickens. When their father came home from work that day, he noticed that the chickens acted kind of strange, kind of topsy-turvy. He got the answer when he walked into the house!

Cleo brought up the name of Clara Luther, the school teacher, and I guess she just wanted to know how many of our readers remember her?

Before her paternal grandmother was married, she, too, taught school. Her name then was Alice Mell, and she lived with two other ladies that liked to smoke their pipes. The smell of that smoke bothered Alice, because it would get into her hair and she didn't want the students to think that she smoked. There was only one way to cure that and that was to wash her hair nightly, which, of course, made her hair-do kinky and frizzy!

After Alice was married, she had two sets of twins. There were neighboring schools that were after her to teach, but she felt that all those twins would keep her busy. The Dutch Corners School was persistently after her, and after much thought, she became their teacher. But that's not the end of the story. Her husband made a double cradle for the last set of twins, who were to accompany their mother to school every day, and her students adjusted very nicely to this atmosphere. I just can't picture this happening today!

Since this particular farm had cats all over the place, many of them had to be de-wormed. The children gave them the medication, alright, which was to be followed by some caster oil according to the directions, which were not read, and as a result most of the cats "hit the dust". Cleo, since then has always remembered to make sure to read the directions!

One more thing. She recalls the days when her father would pick up all the apples and pears from the ground, and take them to Sumnerville to be processed into cider. This is when she told me that pears make red vinegar.

It was such a treat speaking to this great story teller, as it surely brought me "back to the good ol' days".

THE TUNNEL THAT COLLAPSED

Did you know that back in 1883 Berrien Springs was a County Seat, and like most courthouses, there would be a "slammer" in the same compound? I personally can't picture this small community being a seat of government affairs, but a set it was and not an impenetrable one.

I would like to tell you a story about a jail break that occurred in Berrien Springs near the turn of the 19th Century. One wouldn't conceive of such a thing happening in this peaceful town. Perhaps in Al Capone's time, yes, which came some time later. The County Jail was attached to the sheriff's house. Its original design was to hold twenty-four inmates, which in all cases harbored only the less violent. Like most places of confinement, this place, too, was dark, dingy and smelly, and for this reason those who were confined wanted out! I guess everyone knows what kind of weather the month of August brings, and this is when it all happened.

How many prisoners were in jail at the time was not known, but it is clear that eight of them had much time to scheme, to connive, besides what else is there to think about? They definitely wanted to make good their escape.

As originally planned, the jail had an underground cistern directly in the center of the cell block. The cistern furnished water for the prisoners' bath, but it also made a convenient place to begin an escape tunnel. As a rule, this was filled with water and the prisoners pumped it out until they could get into the cistern and begin their work to freedom, which was some twenty feet beyond.

41

The person who knew, or at least who thought he knew, that the outer wall was tunnel-proof, was Sheriff James R. Clark. He thought the foundation extended some eleven feet below the surface, and to the prisoners' delight, it was three and one half feet deep.

There was an air of guilt that permeated the compound the night before, and as a result every single inmate was frisked from head to toe. Nothing suspicious was found. In so many other places of correction, prisoners were always searched for kitchen utensils, from which weapons are made. I know this to be true, as I once had a cousin who worked at the Marquette State Prison in the Upper Peninsula. What he told me is another story.

At the moment though, we're concerned about a great escape from a small town jail. You often wonder what each escapee used to carve his way to sunlight. That night there was nothing confiscated from the inmates, so we presume that they found something to claw their way to the comforts of the real world.

It was Saturday morning and the tunnel was completed. The culprits waited 'til evening for their break. However, something happened during the day. Evidently, the soil was too soft and the tunnel caved in, thus exposing the entire escape route. It was now or never they thought, and so it was now, in broad daylight!

Sheriff Clark discovered the escape shortly, and the chase was on. A posse formed within minutes and the townsfolk were all alerted. The sheriff was first to snare one, and Deputy Will Graham corralled two more, and Deputy Andrew Mars cornered three. Remember this was a small town, and everyone got into the act! There weren't too many houses to begin with to hide from the law, but the forest made good cover. Two did hit the trails of the bush, one of whom was arrested in the State of Vermont, and the other was never captured, though hunted like a snowshoe rabbit.

Of course, there was much excitement in Berrien Springs, as people came from other parts of the Midwest to see the collapsed tunnel. It is now well over a hundred years since this episode took place, and I still wonder what ever happened to that clump of dirt that a lady from Niles took from the tunnel and carried it home?

While we're on the subject of prison breaks, I must tell you of one that happened at Marquette, Michigan in the middle 50's. Believe me, these were not petty larcenists, nor men of simple disorderly conduct, but these were mean desperadoes each carrying a life sentence. There were two that were arrested shortly after their escape from the State Prison, and as the days passed, the others camped along State and Federal Highways keeping a sharp eye on the law, and at the same time feasting on chickens and eggs taken from neighboring farmers. Everyone in the County was alerted about their escape and told that they were armed and considered dangerous. At the time I was living in a small town just south of Marquette, and I remember very distinctly that I went to bed with my 30-30 Winchester beside me. I learned the next morning that the killers passed through during the night. I dreamt about this incident for many years, and wondered what I would have done, had they stormed the door? After a few years I was told that all prisoners were accounted for except one, who eluded the State Police for several years, but he eventually perished in a gun battle with the authorities of the State of Oregon.

In my research I am grateful to the Historical Sketches of Berrien County for giving me the idea to tell you about Berrien Springs.

EAU CLAIRE'S BANK BANDITS

Berrien County was not the quiet and peaceful place as one may have thought it to be. You must keep in mind that this was once Al Capone's haven, Berrien Springs to be more specific. I was always told that this county is the fruit belt of Michigan. With the abundance of fruit came also many dividends. Why this Italian came to these parts is anybody's guess. It could be that he was gathering riches, or it could be that he was looking for recruits to work in and belong to his rapidly growing empire. In 1929 there was an incident that occurred at Stevensville that may have been triggered by the Chicago gang. It seems that all roads along the shores of Lake Michigan were headed toward Berrien County. This little farming community was jolted by the murder of one of its policemen, Charles Skelly, by name. The perpetrator of this crime was a very shrewd operator, and he had a litany of aliases that confused the judicial system. But the law finally did catch up with him and he was later sentenced to life imprisonment.

Not too many miles from Lake Michigan, the people of Eau Claire had something to talk about for a long time. On April 4, 1922, a typical spring day, especially pleasant for the farmers, but most disturbing for the employees of the Eau Claire State Bank.

It was mid-morning when two armed men entered the bank and held the president at bay, and of course, Homer Hess complied with the order. As he walked over to the other employees, who were also held up by the second bandit, he tripped accidentally, which alarmed his captor. Some shots were fired that grazed Hess' stomach. This is when some passersby heard the commotion and set off their own alarm.

Perhaps a week or so before the robbery, the four hardened rascals already got themselves into trouble by stealing a Pratt touring car from Elkhart, Indiana. No doubt this tiny village was on their itinerary, and so they thoroughly canvassed the main roads and thoroughfares, plus all the back roads, thus making all escape routes chartered.

On the day of the robbery this same touring car with the other two henchmen sitting in it, was parked just outside the bank. Everything happened so quickly that they took only part of the loot, which amounted to $1,185. The other satchel containing about $3,000 still lay in the bank. The gangsters sped off with the deputy in hot pursuit and his pistol smokin' at the same time.

In the meantime Mrs. Claxton, the chief telephone operator of this farming town, had every single wire "red hot". Since everyone was alerted and grabbed their shootin' irons, there was a war goin' on, revolver fire against shotgun blasts. Remember this was back in 1922, when all the roads were gravel, and the shoulders of the roads were extremely treacherous. In trying to pick up some speed, not only were the bandits fish-tailing down the roadway, so were the pursuers, and besides all this, there were bullets flying, plus much profanity.

As the race was approaching a tamarack swamp, the lead car and the money and the culprits all landed in a mud hole. In another minute there was another race, and this one was on foot. More gunfire ensued, and I do mean they were blazin' away, until the four came out of the swamp with their hands up. All four being from Gary, Indiana, and the undoubtedly that they had stayed there instead of clomping through the wet mosquito infested piece of real estate.

After it was all over, the four machos spent the next thirty years of their life in a place they swore they would never see.

Maybe they all had a chance to call their relatives and friends and tell them, "Guess what? I've got some good news and some bad. The good news is that I am not hurt, and the bad news is that I am going to jail." This happened about seventy years ago, and I wonder how many readers out there remember this battle in the tamarack swamp?

Ever since the Chicago Gang set foot in this territory people kept vigil for many years. A year doesn't go by without someone talking about the St. Valentine's Massacre, the murders, the bank robberies, as they all had some bearing on the violent reign of one man.

I owe a great deal of gratitude to Robert C. Myers, who arranged the Historical Sketches of Berrien County, and from which I was able to compose my episode.

WANDERER AT 90

In the Northeast corner of the State of Arkansas at the foothills of the Ozarks lived the Kells. There were nine children born to J. R. and Martha Kell, seven boys and two girls. Our happy wanderer at the moment is William, whose home has been in Niles for the past sixty-eight years. "What is his age?," you ask Just about everyone in town knows that he is four score and ten years old. He just had a birthday about two weeks ago, and I heard that while he was at the Post Office on his birthday, some friends started singing "Happy Birthday", and the clerks also chimed in. Now that we have established the age of this man, let's pursue other avenues of this pioneer.

The name Kell, of course, is quite a famous name, especially if you're a sports fan. Do you remember George Kell, the third baseman for the Detroit Tigers, back in the 40's and 50's? Since then he is now a Hall of Famer, and TV broadcaster for the Detroit Tigers. The person about whom we are writing today is an uncle to the famed ballplayer. I asked Bill if his nephew ever stops in to see him, and Bill answered, "Oh, yes, sometimes when he is broadcasting a game from Comiskey Park, he'd stop by at the depot, which is almost in my back yard.

Back in Arkansas when he was a young lad, he would help his sister with the house chores, while his other brothers were out in the field with their father. His folks were religious people. "Every Sunday night," Bill would say, "my sister would play the organ and we'd sing hymns." He went on to say that everybody was happier then, all the neighbors were good, we used to work together and help each other out. He remembers walking about three miles to school. He said, "There was a creek near the school, and each time it rained hard, the creek would swell. My father would come to get us with his team of horses and saddle us across the water." While he was at school he played a lot of baseball, usually center field, he also played hard while he lived in Niles. He talked about the Bierwagens being good ball players.

Bill has always been a barber here in town. He remembers back in the 30's one could get a shave, haircut, shampoo and a massage for $1.50, and during the Great Depression, it was "shave and a haircut two bits." He is the proud owner of 50 different colored State Barber licenses, which he said were on display in our local museum.

By the way, he still loves to drive his car around town, and would you believe back and forth to Arkansas? His daughter doesn't favor this idea, though. This guy looks like a real "sport". They say that he wears a tie just about every day. He did just that while I was there. I guess this is why he looks so sporty! I did notice that he likes his little rocker, rocking with little jerky motions all the while we spoke together. He had a smile that wouldn't stop, and that told me something. At 90 I was trying to see a face spent with age, but that was not to be and his mind was just as sharp.

Bill lost his spouse and great companion about two years ago, for whom he had the greatest admiration. He wrote the following poem in her honor:

> Dear"Kid", when I am all alone
> I see you in every room at home
> Sitting on the porch by an empty chair,
> It's hard to realize you are not there.
> And look over to see if you're by my side
> Every year was precious, I remember

From January to December
While holding your hand, looking thru tears
I try to remember the past sixty six years
So, loved one rest in peace and quiet,
And someday we will reunite.

This man of small stature has, I am sure, a big supply of memories to pass around. I am beginning to be deeply moved when I see some of our senior citizens ignored. "They're just too old to know anything" is the voice of those who propose to come up with some empty answers. I do not hesitate to say that our today's subject would be able "to strike dumb the many contentious people".

To reach this covetous age of 90 and still be able to walk, think, laugh, and drive to Arkansas and back is truly an admirable accomplishment.

The foregoing story that you have just read was recorded back in '91. Today this happy wanderer is 97. His friends and relatives tell me that he still manages to drive his car around town and stops in to visit them. One thing he misses most though, is driving to his beloved state of Arkansas. At this ripe old age, it is incredible that he still manages to maintain that beautiful sense of humor.

It would be such a remarkable feat that this notable person reached the Third Millennium.

AN HISTORIAN PAR EXCELLENCE

This outstanding man of history was born on January 30, 1897, in Mravince, a suburb of Split in Dalmatia, which is a Province of Croatia on the Adriatic Coast. His elementary schooling took place at this home, after which time he attended the classical gymnasium, which is a special school preparatory to the university.

Fr. Victor Rogulj entered the seminary at Ljubljana, the Capital of Slovenia. He studied his philosophy on the island of Cres in the northern Adriatic Sea. His theological studies took place at the University of Innsbruck in Austria. Undoubtedly, this is where he not only excelled in theology, but also in Latin and Greek and other languages and in European History. While at the University he joined the Conventual Franciscan Order, wearing the black clerical habit, distinguishing him from the brown Franciscan. He was ordained a priest on March 19, 1921.

Shortly after his ordination he returned to the seminary of his province, where he became professor of history, geography and the Croatian Language. During this time he also taught religion in the public schools in the vicinity of Belgrade.

This newly ordained cleric came to America in July of 1931, settling at Ambridge, PA. to help organize a Croatian Parish. Being well versed in the Croatian Language, there were several other places in the United States that needed his services.

The Copper Country, which is the uppermost part of Upper Michigan, was well represented by the immigrants from Croatia. The parishioners of St. John the Baptist Church at Calumet were fortunate indeed to have Fr. Victor as their pastor. The appointment was effective in 1939. He was also in charge of the Sacred Heart Mission at Ahmeek.

It was during his stay at Calumet that I had the good fortune of learning more of my parents roots and getting a better understanding of the Croatian Language. Being a novice in the study of Latin, I was very much enlightened by this intellectual linguist.

I distinctly recall his Sunday homilies, which were extremely guttural, but most inspiring. When he was transferred by his Conventual Order in 1952, the Croats of this tiny village and the people of Ahmeek were saddened indeed. After his departure it was rather obvious that his robust stature and disciplined mind was greatly missed. It was not until 1971 that my family learned that he was stationed at St. Jerome's Parish in Detroit. We were honored to be invited to attend Fr. Victor's Fiftieth Anniversary of his ordination to the Holy Priesthood.

It didn't take me too long to look at this man of wisdom and wonder how many minds he molded and how many souls he saved. During our visit we talked about the past, of course, then thought about what was to be. He didn't show his age, nor did he lose that vim and vigor of expression. I believe that was his trademark.

During the early siege of Croatia, the ancient city of Dalmatia was relentlessly pounded by the enemy. At the moment I am not certain whether this man of God was living at the time, but we do know, however, that he returned to his much beloved country, when he retired. There wasn't the slightest question that he was well versed in religion, history and languages. This maker of the modern mind was intellectually blessed. Everyone who knew him was greatly affected when it was learned that he had the misfortune of losing his eyesight.

51

Had Fr. Victor been living today, I must tell you most emphatically that he would have been deeply pained by the continuous war clouds over the country that he passionately cherished.

Those of us who once lived under his jurisdiction, still hold this Innsbruck graduate in high regard. He was not a worldly man, but truly a man of the world. I am most certain that all the places that he touched, his name is synonymous with grace and brilliance. As he himself was so blessed with a special charisma, so we as his subjects were also blessed.

COMING FROM THE LAND OF BRIDGES AND
CHURCHES

Would you believe that I interviewed the first Senior Beauty Queen ever in Berrien County's Apple Festival? She was born a Hoosier in Logansport, Indiana.

As mentioned previously in my writings, these wonderful senior citizens have so much to tell us about themselves, where they were born, what they did, where their parents were born, and so many other interesting things. I want you to know that they're so eager to tell someone about themselves. I really can't understand why one would shun the companion-ship of an older person, when they have so much to tell us, so why not take a few moments to listen to what they have to say. Eunice Stephens is the gracious lady who told me her story today. She lives with all the other nice people of Four Flags Plaza. These people are so glad to be alive and to share their rich experience. For some reason or other in my opinion their wisdom far surpasses the big guns of today.

In the course of our meeting Eunice did not hesitate to expound about her heritage, namely, that her maternal grandparents hailed from County Cork, Ireland. She emphasized about her father's brother being in the Civil War, and likewise her mother's older brother. Her mother's father came from Virginia, whose father was a slave owner.

It interested me in particular how her people came to Indiana. These interviews with these prolific people have certainly broadened my knowledge of geography. Her father's lineage had its roots in Erie, Pa. They pioneered down the canal to Logans Port, which today is Logansport, flanked by the Wabash and Eel Rivers. The town was well known for its Bridges and Churches. The townsfolk also boasted about their railroad trade. Back in the early days the area did produce an abundance of corn, rye and oats, but not any soybeans, which at that time was never heard of.

She recalls when her parents operated a Summer Resort at Lake Cicott, founded by Pierre Cicott. The passenger train ran through these parts, at which time it stopped to let people off at the resort's siding. Since she spent most of the summer months at the lake, she enjoyed swimming the most.

Mrs. Stephens contended that people then cared more for each other than today's populace. She remembers vividly during the flu epidemic when the doctor would come by horse and buggy daily to visit the seven members of her family who were all quarantined. Groceries were needed, however, so her father would put money in the mailbox for someone to pick up the food supplies. Incidentally, their mail was delivered by a carrier who came by motorcycle with a side car. My mother liked that so much, that she would ask him for a ride. Uncle Sam's quick reply would be, "It's against the law!"

I was told that some time in 1914 my father with his horse and buggy went to meet his son at a Pennsylvania depot. On their return trip they stopped to buy a car, which at that time neither of them knew how to drive the machine. After taking several turns at the vehicle, they finally arrived at home to find their mother shocked by their purchase. With all the excitement there was still something that had to be returned—the horse and buggy!

At age four and a half I remember having an aunt at Fresno, CA., whose husband worked at a gold mine at Quincy, CA. They used to go there by stage coach. There was a big lumber camp in that area.

In 1926 my husband worked at the Niles Railroad Hump.

54

It got pretty lonesome when he was gone, so I was hired at the Hilderbrand Hotel. I was twenty years old then. Business at the hotel was very good, especially the restaurant. Since I used to go to work rather early in the morning, the local police entrusted me with a daily chore, and that was to turn off the city street lights every morning. Everybody called me "little Steve". My husband was called "big Steve".

The Hilderbrand had the distinction of having such people as Dr. Bonine and Mr. Vincent Bendix, whom I had both the pleasure of serving. Eunice told me about an amusing incident that happened there one day. There was an old man and lady that came in to see Dr. Bonine, and while they waited, and since it was lunch time, they spread their own prepared lunch on one of the tables. She even poured them coffee. She remembers the day that she met the person who used to sing the Philip Morris commercial on the radio. Remember, "Call for Philip Morris"? She thought that he was just a kid, but found out later that he was old enough to be served a drink!

She remembers Franky's Restaurant in its early days, when she often reminded Franky to spruce his place up a bit. Frank said to her one day as she entered his premises, "You know, Eunice, every time you stick your nose in here, it costs me more money." It seems that he was forever repairing his eatery.

DONAL FAUT, OUR EARLY DAIRYMAN

In my search for stories of the good ol' days, I am amazed to learn just how many people wish to share their life's experiences. Then again there are those who close their ears when asked about the past. In all these groups we have so many different professions, vocations and careers. It is such a joy for me to listen to all facets of life.

Today's subject I found in a coffee shop. Some months ago in the course of another's conversation, I overheard the word "milkman". That was my key to pursue this thought. Frankly, I often wondered what the life of a dairyman would be. I introduced myself to Donal Faut, and he did likewise. It was some time later that we talked about his work back in the 40's.

He and his wife Donna have been married for fifty-two years, and I dare say that they weren't all years of bliss. People have told me that one must live a life of many concerns and hardships to reach that pinnacle. One of Donal's concerns was delivering milk in Valparaiso, Indiana. In this University city he always carried quarts, pints and half pints of milk, and they always clinked! He worked for Holzer's Dairy for three years. He loved his work, but he wasn't too pleased about the employer, who was pretty stingy about giving his employees an occasional day off. In his many associations with the townsfolk, he told me about the time a lady customer who wanted to go on a two-week vacation, but needed someone to take care of her Great Dane dogs. Being that Donal was such a likeable gent, she asked him for the favor, and while doing so, she said that just before feeding time, he could go to the local butcher shop to pick up some bones and meat scraps. This he did very faithfully and religiously, and his reward was twofold. First, a painting that she had mastered as a hobby, and secondly, a Great Dane pup. Mr. Faut did treasure the painting, as he thoroughly enjoyed the work of art. The dog, I wasn't too sure about, so I just let it be. He took great pleasure in helping people, as this one day he even helped a lady hang clothes.

Back then the doors were always open for him. Once he opened the door, he placed the milk in refrigerators, which were cooled by huge chunks of ice. He would often leave the milk on the table, and his money would be there. Many times it was left outdoors before the winter months, and in some cases the money would be there, too. Trustworthy people in the good ol' days! People's doors were always left unlocked. Today some have latches installed. While still living in Indiana, he would often start working at 2 a.m. until 9 a.m. followed by a breakfast, and then back to work. It was at this time that he collected monies that his customers had owed him. Being a young man and trying to make ends meet, he worked part-time in Greek restaurants as a cook. He also told me that one time he worked as a cook at Notre Dame. Little wonder now that he still enjoys cooking.

After he left the confines of Valparaiso, he moved to Niles where he was employed by the Producer's Dairy Co. Don was with this Company for three years, then worked for the Wilson's and Anderson's Dairy at Buchanan. It was here that he delivered milk, usually ½ pints to the workers at Clark Equipment Co. Wouldn't it be a real big lift if we could once again hear that Clark's would be in full operation?

I was rather surprised to learn that in this city in the course of years, there were eight different dairies, though not in operation simultaneously. For your information here is a list: Producer's, City Dairy, Niles Creamery, Victory, Exner's, Singer's, Rice's and Forgerger's. Today, Berrien County does not have a single one, and in the State of Michigan, I was told, there are two or three. Most of our dairy products are processed in the State of Indiana.

Donal tells me there was a day when he was stalled in a ditch that crossed the roadway. It was a local wrecking crew that freed the truck. Since he didn't have any money on his person to pay them, they accepted some buttermilk and chocolate milk as an alternative. He recalls the many days that farmers had several milkers that would take care of the herd. There was no question that because of some farming problems, the milk would often be delayed coming to the dairies.

I am certain that being out on the streets, avenues and byways at that early hour certainly aroused many sleeping dogs in the neighborhood. I imagine that his arrival was like a morning alarm. Being out that early in the fresh air must have given him a clean bill of health. Wouldn't your life today be more fulfilling, if you could still hear the clip clop of the horse's hooves on some cobblestone, knowing that it was your milkman? Maybe it would still be rewarding just to hear the clinking of the milk bottles! But for thirty-seven years Donal couldn't keep those bottles quiet! Today he has the distinction of being one of the early birds in the milk business.

I guessed easily that this man does not know the meaning of boredom. His many hobbies range from cooking to carpentry, from artistry to needlework. What else can be said than to state that his versatility is certainly to be admired.

THE IMMIGRANT MOTHER

I had the occasion to visit a nursing home the other day
and I couldn't help but look at the many mothers that have
been confined to this place of weak bodies and twisted minds.
Some cannot walk, some are completely bedridden, some just
shuffle along, some just sit and stare, some talk, but so in-
coherently. In some, reason for living is almost meaningless.

While I looked at all frailties of life, I was somewhat
troubled that so many of these beautiful people will not even
be aware that America will soon celebrate Mother's Day. What
is more troubling is that some of their kin haven't bothered to
stop in and just look at them, nor touch them. It is very possible that some of these shut-ins were born of immigrant parents. Some weeks ago a very concerned mother of our community sent me a piece of writing that I want you to read. Its title
reads *THE IMMIGRANT MOTHER, THE UNSUNG HER-
OINE AND PIONEER OF AMERICA*. The unsigned article
was found in the Union, a Catholic Fraternal Weekly Newspa-
per. Here are those memorable thoughts:

"For all eternity America is indebted to the immigrant
mother, whether she was English, Hungarian, German, Slovak,
Polish, Russian, Greek, Syrian, Bulgarian, Czech, Irish,
Slovenian or Ukrainian. Born in the old country, she usually
married at a young age the young boy with whom she worked
in the fields. While still a young bride, and sometimes with
child, she remained and waited, while her man left for America, that distant land filled with promises of a better life.

The days, months, and sometimes years passed slowly,

59

while she patiently waited for word from her husband. Finally, when the letter came with the passage fare for the long boat ride to America, she gathered up her few possessions and children, and boarded the ship to join her husband. She found him working in the steel mills, brick- yards, coal mines, and on the railroads; and she found him living in a shack, shanty, railroad car, or even a tent. But at least this was a start, a foundation of a new life, and here in America, by his side, she prepared for the years ahead.

Our country was young; it needed the laborers; and she gave to America, five, six, or more children of her body, and of her soul. While her husband worked in the bitter cold of winter, or in the blistering heat of summer, in ditches laying sewers, and deep in the ground mining coal or iron ore, she worked from early morning to late at night, cooking at a coal stove, washing her clothes with a washboard, and heating the water in a big copper tub on that same coal stove. At the same time she took care of the children, preparing breakfast, making lunches, and sending them to school.

Now, the freshness of young womanhood is gone. By the flickering oil lamp she sews and irons clothes late into the night. She scrimps and saves to dress her children decently, while she wears an old dress and stays at home. Her children must have an education, so they may be respected and amount to something some day.

And then at last, when her children are grown, as her cup of joy runneth over, we see how want, deprivation and hard-ships have taken their toll. All worn out, her bones aching from so many ills, she lays helplessly in her sick bed, and her children gather around her. She turns to kiss them and to bless them—and then, she is gone. She is the unsung heroine of America. No statue can be built high enough, no marble is precious enough, with which to sculpture a fitting memorial to the immigrant mother.

She, who with her breasts nurtured us, with her arms raised us, with her ideal inspired us, with her tears washed us clean, with her devotion saved us, and then on the altar of love, laid out her worn spent body. . .And from her place in Heaven she sent down her blessing on America, for what America has offered to her children in this great land. May the people of America never forget what they owe to that sweet and blessed soul, the immigrant mother of us all."

Happy Mother's Day, Mom.

THE EARTH WAS CLEAN

I remember when Planet Earth showed me its true colors. It was clean, pure, and sometimes I felt as if it was untouched. I never doubted whether the air that I breathed would cause any harm to me or to my fellow man. I never used to worry whether the water I drank was free from foreign matter. I remember so vividly while playing ball in the wide open fields, I would often pluck tall blades of grass and hold them in my mouth, and never thought for a moment that what I pulled from the earth would be contaminated.

Many times I hunted for wild game, only to find on rare occasions that which I had shot was diseased, not by the hand of man, but by nature's course. Fuel for the automobiles was plentiful and cheap, and the fumes they left behind was really no big concern for us, but now we have multiplied a hundred fold, and so have our fast machines. It is the multitude of these exhausts that baffles the minds of engineers. Man has in truth become a lethal weapon. It seems that what he makes, whether for pleasure or his betterment, may one day be his detriment.

Do you remember the times when you used to eat snow and when your mother tinted it with food coloring, and when she'd put a pinch of vanilla extract in that snowball? It was just like having an ice cream treat. That was yesterday. We're doing just about everything to stay young and exuberant, not realizing that at the same time we are destroying the ozone layer.

I believe we are very much aware about the things that are destroying our environment, even our habitat. What is so disturbing is that the places at which we are employed, are releasing gases that cause us much concern.

There were so many moments in my youth, when walking through forests and virgin timber, that I would only see wind-falls, growing mosses, ferns and countless fungi. Today when I return to those trodden paths of old, I stumble over rubble, rusted cans, bottles and broken glass. As a young adventurer, I really can't remember the number of times I used to cup my hands to get a drink of water from a running brook. This I hesitate to do today, for I find this to be robbing the pattern of my past. However, there is still a mannerism I possess, namely, to pinch any family of the evergreen and smell it to my heart's content. This I will continue to do until the end of my time.

Should man destroy all the trilliums, arbutuses, the ferns, and all the trees and plants that I long to touch and brush, and uproot all the berry bushes, which gave me much fruit, then for me the earth is no more.

I can't help but picture the early American Indian standing and meditating about the earth, which once was his and his alone, and how he was robbed of its beauty and glory. This red-man, who is now bent and spent with age, ponders about all the pleasantries he once had at the banks of the River Ontonagon, fishing, hunting and gathering furs for his hungry and cold people.

He looks at the snow, and that, too, is no longer immaculate. Even the streams and creeks have a different hue. His fishing on the Great Lakes has been somewhat curtailed, but he is still in pursuit of the abundant rabbit, bear, deer and moose.

The Indian that I have portrayed is just an imaginary figure, and I have given him the name of Konteeka, as this was the name I liked best. He is now so dismayed because the white man has blemished the fruits of his land. It is with utmost certainty that those who are to follow him will see more of the same, and even more painstaking.

So many diseases have scourged the earth, some are of great concern to man, who has been trying to desperately to arrest the agony and torment of those who are afflicted.

We know that so many of us who are nearing the end of our race in time, that we would want to see our earth as new and clean as when we began our course in time. It is most certain that future generations will have to have an ingenious plan and work hard to save this place we call home.

LOOKING BACK

There's something special about looking at an antique, at ancient ruins; there's something exceptional about gazing at a find in a glacier; there's something completely fascinating about observing an object on an abandoned farm. There is something absolutely beautiful just looking at a human being.

Today I'd like to take you back to the good ol' days, just simply back then, more specifically fifty years ago, perhaps even seventy years ago, or let's just say as far back as you can remember. Care to guess?

As you know from the past, I do talk about nice things and not so nice things. People tell me all kinds of things, and the people in the media are even showing us how life is really lived in all parts of the world. Some stories about life are even received in the mail, such as I am about to tell you today. This was sent to me by Mrs. Rachel Taipalus, who is now a resident in the State of Florida, but a native of Calumet. This is a story about her husband when he was a young boy about eight or nine years old, also a native of the Copper Country. This incident happened practically within a stone's throw from my birthplace. It must have occurred before my time, as I do not recall the event. I believe that the story was first recorded in September, '82.

Looking back, many families in this tiny village had milking cows roaming about. This part of the episode I remember very well, as my family had a cow that I used to lead to the pasture daily. In certain areas the animals were free to graze anywhere. The boy in our story was an early riser, as he had the chore of looking for the cows. Some of them had bells around their necks, which made it easier to locate them. As he was nearing the edge of a forest, he was horrified to see a man hanging from a limb of a tree. His description was absolutely terrifying, when he stood there watching the body turning and twisting, and each time the rope was being tightened and loosened. Naturally, he forgot about the cows, and ran to the nearest house to announce the gruesome discovery. It was just a matter of minutes that the place was mobbed by gawking people. It was later learned that the victim, after a family quarrel, went to his happy hunting ground by this method.

Do you remember the Prohibition Era, Al Capone and Company in Chicago, The Purple Gang in Detroit? Do you remember all the Blind Pigs that flourished in these cities? I guess we still have them around, and it appears that they are here to stay.

The same fellow who told us about the twisting rope, also gave us some insight about the border patrols on the Detroit river. Those of us who lived in the late 20's and in the 30's, recall the many things that happened in the Motor City. First of all, the Great Depression which left us with countless soup kitchens, unemployment figures that staggered our imaginations. And in the Old World Adolph Hitler was putting Germany back on the map, only to become the power monger of Europe. Our neighboring country, Canada, was free and easy with alcoholic beverages, while the States were dry. This became the smuggling era, by plane, train, boats and underwater scheming. Someone would always find a way to import illegal spirits. I can't imagine what the U.S. Coast Guard, the U.S. Customs Border Patrol were experiencing on the Detroit River to put a stop to this smuggling. Without a doubt there were bullets flying here, too. Even after the Repeal of Prohibition, the Officials at the Border were still busy seizing products, such as face powder, perfumes, bacon and hams, and would you believe, onions, which in the U.S. sold for 30 cents per pound while in Canada they sold for 5 cents per pound?

During WW II things in America were rationed, which meant more illegal food-stuffs. People were even hiding perishables in the hubcaps and motors of their cars. Looking back again, do you remember when kitchen matches were often lit by striking them on the seat of a man's trousers? This was a man's trick, and he also lit a match by striking it on his thumbnail. These were the times when cigarettes were really the fad!

HURLEY WAS ONE OF DILLINGER'S STOPS

Our native from Ironwood tells me that many of the young have left this town, just simply because of lack of employment. This is so evident today, should you walk the main streets. Even the grass in the cracks of the sidewalks are earmarks that not too many care anymore. This is also true in the land of Copper.

I certainly have fond memories of the high school football clashes between Ironwood and Calumet. Those young people from the iron country were humongous. All of those blockbusters hailed from Ironwood's Luther L. Wright High School. By the way, Mr. Stone is a '55 graduate of this school.

Don handed me a couple photos, one of which showed a record snowfall. He wasn't too sure about the year, but that really doesn't matter, as that part of Michigan and also the Copper Country have many record snowfalls! The other photo shows a line of teams of horses and buggies, perhaps a funeral cortege, dating back some time in the early 1900's. In the background several mining hoists are visible.

This tender of legal affairs handed me a printed sheet, showing Gogebic County's Grand View Hospital as its letterhead. The date was August 11, 1937. He had two reasons to smile, when he gave me this information, one, because his mother had just given birth to one of Michigan's attorney to be, and the other reason was the hospital's statement showing the entire bill for a thirteen day stay as $81.90—compare this to today's astronomical figures!

According to this calculation, it was rather interesting to

68

know that the distance from Ironwood across Big Mac Bridge to Detroit, was equivalent to the distance from Detroit to New York City. Also, Ironwood is further west than St. Louis, MO.

During the migration surge, there were many people from Cornwall, England, that settled in Michigan primarily in the Copper and Gogebic Ranges. These Cornishmen, as they were called, were miners of coal and iron back home in Great Britain. They came to America seeking new avenues of wealth and prosperity. It was they who introduced the famed pasty (pronounced as pa stee), which resembles our meat pies. They were also responsible for kidney stew and kidney pies. I remember my father, relatives and friends going to work in the copper mines, carrying such delicacies in their lunch buckets tucked under their arms.

East of Ironwood, some twenty-five miles or so, was an old lumber camp located at Marenisco. There are so many stories about its lumberjacks and about their payroll, most of which are true, perhaps all of them. But I wish I had a penny for every jack for the number of times he invaded Hurley, Wisconsin. You see, this town was a drinking town. What else could it have been with about one hundred saloons on Silver Street? With drinking came "one armed bandits", other forms of gambling, and of course, women and song. If you have never heard this to be so, now you know. These men would barrel into town, and after spending all their hard-earned cash, some walked to the sleds, which their bosses had waiting for them, and some had to be carried. This went on for several months, just as long as the cold and snow held up, for this is what they needed to skid logs.

Hurley was also known as one of John Dillinger's rendezvous. His other big hideout was located in Little Bohemia around the Manitowish Waters. The cabin where he and his gang stayed is still quite well preserved. There is still evidence of his battle with the Feds. He did get away, but he did meet his Waterloo some years later in the Windy City.

The people of Gogebic County are not completely forgotten nor are they forlorn, since the mining boom has ceased. Life and excitement still abound during the skiing season. I venture to say that this area is one of the Midwest's best. The highest ski jump is Copper Peak, from which one can see on a clear day our neighboring country of Canada, and the States of Minnesota and Wisconsin. On this slope we find expert skiers, who perform the art of ski flying. There are other downhill ski areas in the vicinity of Ramsay, Bessemer and Wakefield, namely, Indian Head, Blackjack Mountain and Big Powder Horn. Without a doubt the Norwegians, Swedes and Finns were responsible for America's winter sports. These North Atlantic immigrants showed us the skill of commercial fishing. There is so much that these Europeans left us, not only their sport, but also their culture, their culinary and agricultural expertise, and certainly their staunch and strong faith.

I am indeed indebted to Mr. Stone for shedding much light in my narrative about a county still rich with iron veins, and still richly supplied with beautiful people.

A CHAMPION IN EGG ARTISTRY

This is my first attempt at interviewing an educator. Some months ago I received a complimentary note from a teacher with whom I had taught for several years. In her note was a suggestion that I contact my today's subject for a story. The writer of this letter did assure me that part of her report would bring to light something that had happened in 1942.

Calling Marie Enger for an interview was not easy. Since I have known this dedicated teacher for some time, and knew how she would approach my asking for the interview, I decided that I would be frank and blunt with her. I asked her, "How about tomorrow at 3?" And so it was tomorrow at 3!

Marie was born on a farm in Cullom, Illinois. There were three girls and one boy in the Getz family. She became her father's helper in the fields, even plowing with a team of horses. In so many of my interviews, the stories originate on the farm. I can hardly associate that word with the world of today. While we're on the subject of the fields, Marie brought up something while she was with her father in the cornfield. "Do you hear those bells, Marie?" her father asked. He continued, "I bet that's the end of WWI!" And so it was. When she mentioned bells in the cornfield, I thought of a famous painting entitled, The Angelus, portraying two peasants in prayer in the field, listening to the bells of the country church.

The Getz family drove to church every Sunday with horse and buggy. Marie told me that on many occasions their feet would get cold, even wrapped up with many blankets. Her family was quite religious. She was proud to tell me that some

71

of her relatives became nuns. It was some months ago that a family told me that the head of the household never did go to church, but in today's narrative we have the head of the family who never missed a Sunday. There are those who do, and then there are those who do not, just some food for thought.

Back in Illinois Marie attended St. Joseph Academy, a school taught by some French nuns. Her college years were spent at Illinois State and the University of Illinois. She modestly told me that she had the distinction of belonging to the honor society and the debating team. It was her aim to teach school, which she did for ten years in the State of Illinois. In 1936 she started molding characters in the City of Four Flags in the Old Junior High School, and then finished her career at Ring Lardner Junior High School. As we sat and talked, she had the highest praise for Mr. Zabel, who was the principal of the Junior and Senior High Schools at that time.

Prior to the death of Marie's husband, the late Walter Enger, An Accountant for the Michigan Revenue Department, they traveled to many parts of the Globe. Marie handed me a list of the places they visited, namely, California, Florida, Canada, the New England States, the Caribbean, New Orleans, Washington, Hawaii, Mexico, Scandinavia, Wisconsin, The Upper Peninsula of Michigan, Belgium, Germany, Holland, The British Isles, Spain and Portugal. Her greatest adventure was attending the Passion Play at Oberammergau, Germany.

This teacher of English, now retired, busies herself with many hobbies, such as needlepoint, crewelwork and papier-mache. Her forte, of course, is Egg Artistry. Giving you a complete history of this art is another story, but I will attempt to share with you just a little knowledge of a field that requires much patience. Her collection of eggs consists a great variety, such as turkey, duck, quail, peacock, tinamou, ostrich, rhea, emu, and even a cassawary egg from Australia. The goose egg, too, is one of her specialties, besides, the rhea, which she says, is her favorite. For those of us who know so little about decorating eggs, this artist gave me a couple of clues about this job. The eggs are first punctured carefully at both ends, and then a rod is run through the egg to break the yoke. The contents are blown out with an ear syringe, and the shells are cleaned and allowed to dry for several days. If the egg is stained in this first process, they must then be carefully washed. Of course, there is much more to this business, and I suggest that you consult this famed individual!

Marie told me about her father's new Model T Ford, which was the talk of the town in all parts of America back then. The whole family went for a long ride, about twenty-three miles worth, which took about a half day in those days. All the roads were gravel. Going down this one hill was a breeze, but coming back was a big problem. "My father couldn't make the hill, so he told us to get off while the car climbed the hill," Marie laughed. "We had to walk back up the hill to meet him there," she said. This is why some of us can say, "those were the good 'ol days!"

I must end this story on a sad note. On January 16, 1942, Marie's sister Alice, a stewardess on a TWA Flight, was killed in a plane crash near Las Vegas. The plane was not able to climb to the proper altitude, and as a result plowed into a mountain top. There were sixteen others that died in this mishap, many soldiers and the famous actress Carole Lombard, the wife of Clark Gable. I'm sure that many of our readers will recall this tragedy.

WARMING THE CHILDREN'S FEET

A beautiful memory has stayed with me and always will as it happened when I was a little girl going to a one-room country school. I lived on a farm some distance from our school and walked through fields to get to the road that lead to the school building. During wintertime it was pretty rough walking through snowdrifts in the fields. So many times we were up to our knees, and the snow would go over our galoshes and our feet became very, very cold. Every winter morning at the school there would be a lovely lady there with a little gray in her hair, waiting for all the little children. She had already stoked the big round furnace, which was in the school-room itself. It was very cozy indoors, but our feet were numb with cold. This kind lady would have all of us sit down and one by one she would take off our boots, shoes, stockings, and with her hands she would start to rub our feet until they felt warm again. She would put everything by the furnace to dry. When our stockings and shoes were dry enough, she would have us put them back on our feet, and by the time the other students and teacher would arrive, our school day began. This warm story was submitted by my spouse, Charlene, who is a native of Niles.

STORIES THAT ONE JUST CAN'T FORGET—The other day a gentleman told me that he really liked his mother-in-law. We usually don't hear about such flattery, but he did proceed to tell me why. He enjoyed her stories, and she was only eighty-five years young. You often hear people say, "gee, I wish I had recorded my grandfather's stories. They were so real, so touching." There must be scores out there somewhere in Niles who could sit down with you and tell you stories that would make excellent material for a TV Mini-series. They tell me that at one time Niles was a great railroad center, what could you tell us about that?

A KIDNAPPING AT NILES IN '38

I had the good fortune of seeing Niles on film back in 1938 and at the same sitting I saw what your beauty queen looked like, too, as she arrived at the local train depot. There were all kinds of dignitaries to meet her, men with suits and ties, women with hats and dresses, the very young with caps and knickers. It was truly a different scene from today's apparel.

There was a movie being taken of this celebrity as she smiled and greeted the many guests and residents of this Four Flags City of Niles. It was quite obvious that the people surrounding her were proud, because she just happened to be one of them.

The local merchants sponsored a parade in her honor and what a shindig that was! To begin with there were all kinds of hugs and kisses goin' on. In that big line up were some mounted police, police and motorcycles, big fancy automobiles with some pretty fancy people sitting in them, waving to the many fans gathered along the cobblestone streets. You might have known that the indispensable one-man band Vic Heide would be there, the local Boy Scout Troop was there, too. Of course, the queen was in the best lookin' car of the bunch, waving and touching the hands of the onlookers. In that crowd were youngsters showing off their many breeds of dogs on leashes, bicycles galore ridden by knicker-clad boys. You could see that the high school band was doing its stuff. There was so much to see during the quick revolution of the film reel, that I will let you envision what else one could have seen. However, I will try to record what my memory has retained during those treasured moments.

As I sat and watched what was going on in your city in '38, I just couldn't fathom the many hundreds of people that jammed The Four Flags Hotel, the stores, the churches and the factories. Those of you still living, can you remember your city being that bustling? Then again, who doesn't come out to see a parade with a queen as a main attraction?

I am rather curious to know who the cameraman was on this spectacular day, for his work was most commendable. For all we know this film may be the only one of its kind.

One thing I did notice especially was the number of young men that were smoking cigarettes or cigars. This was particularly noticeable at the Hotel, the depot, the parade, gas stations, and at the many places of work. I guess the women in the era didn't know how to sport cigarettes. It was rather ironic that during the viewing of this film, our nation was advertising a smoke-out!

The particular people that were brought to my attention were the late Richard Warren, a former teacher and Superintendent of the Niles School System, the late Joe Whitwam, the long-time athletic director of the Niles Schools. Other acquaintances, such as Sheridan Cook, George Bishop, and I am sure many others whom I personally did not recognize. There were many factories that were being filmed, and since my spouse had a brother working at the local mushroom plant, we watched closely to see whether he would be coming out of the plant when its workers were dismissed. We were indeed rewarded to see that lean figure come barreling out of the plant with the rest of the crew!

The cameraman scanned many areas of interest, namely, the Ready Theater, Tyler Co., Kawneer, Thayer's Jewelry, Stanner's Electric Service, Thomas Ice Cream Parlor, Kugler's Restaurant, Niles Laundry, Michigan Mushroom Plant, Oldsmobile Garage, Babitt Lumber Co., Contois Hardware, Bear

Cat and Moskins. Are you familiar with all of them?

During all the beautiful festivities, the handshakes, the kisses, the laughter, the smiles, there were other sinister things going on in the back alleys and hideouts of the city. There were desperadoes lurking about to kidnap the queen. On two separate occasions the kidnappers did mistakenly take two young ladies as the queen. On the third attempt, however, they were successful, but their escape was short-lived, as the law stepped in and captured the would-be-captors. During the viewing of the film, I was told that the real queen sat within three arm's lengths from our sitting. I must tell our readers that our movie actors and actresses were all spectacularly staged.

It is most regrettable, however, that most of the actors depicted in this remarkable film and most of the adults pictured have all gone to their eternal reward. R.I.P.

One last comment to the many readers of this footage, the film, indeed, is a classic, and I would highly recommend that you see it. And while you're watching, you just may happen to see a relative or friend, and who knows, maybe you'll see 'YOU'.

COTTONTAIL RUNWAY

Brothers III, Randy, Bobbie and Clint Cordell and his son John had been planning a rabbit hunt for several months. As luck would have it, they chose a day in late January. The sun was bright and warm and the ground was covered with soft melting snow. The hunters all piled into their pickups and headed for the briars, brush piles and the tall grass. Most owners of trucks during the winter months place concrete blocks in the bed of their machines, as this would help for better traction. Clint's bunch was no exception, but his looked like he was headed due north to the Alaskan Highway.

It didn't take you too long to reach the rabbit runways outside the city limits of Kalamazoo. As soon as you opened one of the truck doors, somebody yelled, "There goes one!" Somehow you had a feeling that a bag limit was forthcoming.

I'm still a novice at hunting cottontails, but I do know that they're experts in zigzagging. Getting a bead on these fleeting targets is not easy. You had your chance on the first one, but in all your excitement, you squeezed the trigger and all you heard was a "click"—the chamber was empty!

What a day for stalking those furred critters! It was just a matter of minutes that all of you manned your positions, sneaking through the briars, brush piles, slashings, mounds of tall grass and what all. One of you kicked the brush pile, then the shootin' started. This was now a war zone, rabbits were flying all over the place, tearing across small ravines, swales and all sorts of flat country. Sure there were some misses, but it really didn't matter, as there were other pieces of real estate around the next forty that was still untouched.

I wonder what would have happened, had you hunters taken along a couple of beagles, and as you well know that the bark of a beagle is music to a hunter's ear. From the looks of things, you would have had a lot of music, loud and clear. But then their barking would push the rabbits into their holes. This is what makes the cottontails so much different than their cousins, the snowshoe hare, which will circle for hours.

Your memorable photos tell us that you must have emptied several boxes of ammo. Looked like Clint was carrying some pieces of hardwood readied for the camp's kitchen cook stove! Of course, you nimrods were well aware that you left a few cottontails hiding in their tunnels. All in all though, it was a hunt that you'll be talking about for years to come.

Now you're back home defrosting your prize, getting them ready for a pot roast, or better still a rabbit stew. The French Indian rabbit hunters from Mackinac County had a recipe, whose taste was out of this world!

In case you're still wondering where these runways are located, just ask Clint up on the second floor of our local Lakeland Medical Center.

Not Bad for a Day's Run

A DESIGNER'S PARADISE

Our beginnings are truly unique, one of us having our roots at the bottommost section of Southwestern Michigan, namely, Niles, the Four Flags City, and the other, a native of Calumet, the center of the Copper Country, at the top of the Upper Peninsula.

In early 1956 we began our life in Milwaukee, Wisconsin, where we were employed until the spring of '57. It was at this time, that Charlene's brother, Ted Miswick, called us from his home at Brevort, and stated that he needed help to operate his newly constructed restaurant. You might say that this was quite an opportune moment for us to go "back home". It took us about a week or so to get organized to move lock, stock and barrel to the Miswick settlement.

Ted's Motel and Restaurant were located of U.S. #2 West, some twenty miles from the Straits of Mackinac, which then ferried passengers on Lakes Michigan and Huron connecting the main lands of the Lower and Upper Peninsula.

Much of the tourist trade helped the owners of motels and various eateries. Since there was an influx of tourists, Ted was in dire need of someone to take care of his business.

Our work in the restaurant was really something new and certainly a challenge. However, in due time our routine became a pleasure. It was getting to be physically impossible for us to do all the cooking and waiting on tables, so we hired waitresses who lived in the vicinity.

In the fall of '57 one of the World's Wonders, the Mackinac Bridge, was opened to automobile traffic going to and from both peninsulas. Our business flourished then, and this is when we decided to purchase the premises. It was at this point that different shifts were needed in our work, thus necessitating a bigger working force. The new recruits were all residents of Niles, and it was just a matter of time that these novices adjusted themselves to this new life style.

Our first child, a daughter Kathleen, was born on April 15, 1959. Needless to say, that this was a blessed event. We recall taking care of her in a small room, which was just off the restaurant's kitchen. The three of us lived under these conditions for a short period, until we moved into Charlene's sister Jean's home.

Since our business picked up considerably, we contemplated having a new house built, overlooking Lake Michigan, just a stone's throw from Jean's place. With Charlene's musical background came her artistic abilities to design, and for this reason I came up with the title of a designer's paradise.

Her brother Ted, a self-educated master builder didn't waste any time to begin clearing the land and excavating the site for our new residence. It was in early fall of '59 that construction was in full swing, and through Ted's maneuvering that I became his novice builder, plumber and electrician. Had it not been for him, there would have been many things undone as time went on in our lives.

The advent of another deer season was beginning to show by the heavy traffic just below our frame building. Along came Charlene's brother's friends from Niles who were all avid hunters. When the season opened in earnest, those who were lucky enough to bag their game, had the pleasure of hanging their prize within the indoor skeleton of our house, more precisely, along the hallway. I distinctly remember working in the building and warming myself by a homemade stove designed by Ted from a 50 gallon oil drum. I may have had some experience about this setup, as my brother had a similar make-shift in his hunting camp. At any rate the one we have in mind was located near where the present entrance is to the sunken living room.

We worked on the house during the winter months, and because of our untiring efforts, the house on the bluff was completed the following summer. Ted and I were quite proud to have dug our own well, and from this water source we installed the heating system. I'm sure that there have been some alterations since then, but the hot water heat still comfortably permeates this house of treasured memories.

On December 6, 1961, our son Michael was born. Charlene and I have such vivid memories of bringing him home, not as a very healthy child, but an infant experiencing his first head cold, one which most of us seriously doctor.

Winters in this part of Michigan are long and sometimes vicious. On this one clear winter day looking out into the frozen lake, I noticed some dogs in hot pursuit of a coyote. I watched this chase until they were out of sight.

After Labor Day our business was closed and had been until the following Memorial Day. We were beginning to sense that our activity in the restaurant was slackening, which was due to the building of other eateries a shorter distance from the Mackinac Bridge. Naturally, this was a big blow to our livelihood, and in due time we were forced to relinquish our operations.

We moved to Niles, and after some months of graduate studies through extension courses at Notre Dame, Michigan State and Western Michigan, I joined the Education Field teaching English, Michigan History and Latin.

After our departure from the confines of Mackinac County, our home was temporarily occupied, until its present occupants by the name of Owen and Barbara Jorgensen, who have made it their permanent residence.

Before we tell you about our life on this beautiful knoll, here are the original descriptions of this cozy place. The home was comprised of seven rooms, starting with Utility, Kitchen, Living Room, a Bath and three Bedrooms. During our short stay we had the pleasure of having some of our waitresses sharing our dwelling place.

At this time we would like to tell you about some of the incidents that occurred by and around our house, incidents which Charlene and I still harbor in our hearts and minds. Naturally, they concern our growing children—the day that Kathleen disappeared and was found approaching Highway U.S. #2, then suddenly stopped, watched and listened to her mother's miraculous call. This was just another moment when God was good to us. Today our daughter is 36 and the mother of three boys. Then the many days that our son would make his daily runs over to his Aunt's house to see if any more blueberries had ripened overnight. He is 34 now and very versatile in so many things. Majoring in Biology he is one of the keepers of the Zoo at Royal Oak, Michigan, and as a thrilling hobby he is licensed to operate a small airplane.

Another incident which I have also recorded in my collection of writings is the night that Charlene's brother Jim rapped on our bedroom window in the wee hours of this mid-January morning. We can still hear him yelling, "They're coming!" We knew exactly what he meant, as he talked about his barn creatures over the next knoll. Wrapping ourselves with warm jackets, scarves, mitts, boots and what all, we hurried on some new crunchy snow until we came to the place of the newly born piglets. Today we tell people not to smoke, but believe me, Jim was smokin' up a storm that day! Besides this manger-like appearance, there were other animals other than the sow and her brood, there were other hogs, a cow and a horse. Outdoors was bitter cold, so much so, that you noticed body heat escaping from the animals. We helped Jim in the "delivery room". The world welcomed seventeen piglets. Charlene and I still talk about this on many cold nights. Since Jim's passing, she and I are the sole survivors of these treasured moments and memories.

We still manage to travel these parts, to visit, to camp and tease the scrappy trout at Little Brevort River. Perhaps one of the warmest visits in recent memory, was the day that Dave Movalson informed us about the present owners of our house. They wanted to meet us. And so it happened that we drove up this very familiar place and introduced ourselves to the Jorgensens. We had kind of a feeling that Dave told them that we were on our way. This was one short stopover that Charlene and I will never forget. We could tell that these happy people were proud to show us their home. We were indeed pleased to have met two artists, one a musician and the other that excelled in portrait painting and other designs.

We left this house being reassured that we will meet once again, and they wanted us to stay "at your old new home".

VETERAN SAILOR WWI

Several months ago I was fortunate to have received some correspondence dating back to 1918. My nephew, Andrew Munsell informs me that while he was rummaging through some of his mother's memorabilia, he came across some WWI letters that were written by our brother during his hitch in the U.S. Navy in France. Andrew knew that I had been busy with memories and records, so his uncle came to mind. It was a joy to read these writings, as during the close of that War, I was just an infant. I was rather amazed about his penmanship, and even now I recall during his lifetime his writing was noticeably well written.

While my brother was in the Service, his correspondence was sent to his oldest sister, and to our parents. Here are some of his thoughts: "Dear Sis, I wish you, your hubby and children good health and happiness, and see to it that Vicky keeps up her piano lessons, as I expect her to be a good player when I come home (Vicky is Andrew's mother). Tell Ma that I attend Sunday mass regularly. I'm sure that she must be proud to have two sons in the Service. I am beginning to learn the French Grammar, and the French people. Of course, I miss that Milwaukee Schlitz 5 cents a glass beer." The sailor continues to tell his dad to take good care of that Model T, and asks him to send him some peerless and chocolates. "I heard from my brother Steve who is a cooking doughboy in Berlin. How is the garden doing? Love to everyone at home, especially baby Edward." (The author of this book is that baby Edward).

When both of my brothers returned from active duty, they

got their first look at their new brother. This addition to our family made it an even dozen! As an adolescent their own families became a part of our family. We were very close to each other. When we were at play, they would often take the time to tell me about their fathers' exploits while serving in Uncle Sam's Army.

Being of Slavic descent, our sailor's first name read Ladislav. However, since this became difficult for the majority of the townspeople to pronounce, he chose the name of Lodi, which he held for the remainder of his life. In due time his family name was also Anglicized, thus giving it a more English appearance.

The name U.S. became a major part of his life, as he chose his career in life to work for the U.S. Post Office. He was assigned as a rural carrier driving a horse-drawn rig. During WWII he published a newsletter which he sent to thousands of servicemen. The letter was entitled, "Til we meet again, Buddy". He also busied himself with a radio program known as "Lodi's Oldtimers".

I have fond memories of him as being a God-fearing man, a respected father, a joy to be with at a deer hunting camp, and possessing a camaraderie to be admired.

As a final gesture, I, the baby brother wish to make a personal salute to my brother, and WWI Veteran Sailor.

HUNTERS OF THE PLAINS OF SANDS

Brisk November winds and killing frosts are exciting reminders of the advent of a very special season—the season of Big Game hunting. The smell of leaves, the cold, the rain, the snow, call men to reminisce, to talk, laugh, plan, to think and to dream.

Even the Canadian Honkers are telling the surveyors of the wilds, that it's time to head for the hardwoods, the pines and hemlocks, the ridges, swales, the knolls, the streams and swamps, the logging roads, the trails and tote roads. It has become an obsession for you. Should we call it November madness?

The other day I had a warm and exceptional visit with three elderly gentlemen, two brothers and their brother-in-law. I made it a special point to interview these people. You see, they had just returned from their annual deer hunt in the Upper Peninsula of Michigan, more precisely from the plains of Sands. They emphatically told me that this was their final run, and frankly stated that old age had set in, which for obvious reasons hampered their fighting the elements. Fifty-six years of continuous deer hunting had taken its toll.

The eldest of this trio was Bob Groat, whom, I might add, was proud of his ninety years. Next in line was his brother-in-law, Fred Franz, who sported a big smile, when he said, "And I'm eighty-eight." The youngster in the group was Bob's brother, Ben, who is eighty-seven, which spelled a total of two hundred and sixty-five years.

Once they started to tell me about their life in the wilds,

there was no stopping them. Ben is the literary buff in this relationship. Fred is the Big Game enthusiast. This is when he took out his wallet and flashed some photos about his trophies that he had brought down in years past, such as polar bears, grizzlies, brown and black bears, musk ox, and an owl that resembled some prehistoric specimen. He mentioned that purchasing a license for hunting polar bears had an astronomical tag. And finally, Robert, who had a special avocation, that the other two could not muster. He was a builder of replicas of renowned buildings. Believe me, he was quite proud to point out a replica of his birthplace.

For the reader who is not familiar with the territory named, Sands, may I suggest that you look at Michigan's Upper Peninsula, and locate the city of Marquette along the shores of Lake Superior. Looking just south you will see the 'hallowed' grounds of Sands. These are the plains that are so memorable to these three pioneers of the wild kingdom.

"We all started going up there in the early 40's," they said. "This was hardwood country then, it was a lonesome and noiseless place until Uncle Sam built his Sawyer A.F.B." Bob remarked that he used to see Air Force people walking the logging roads looking for the elusive white tail. "We'd make a lot of drives on foot and also by car, and some of those roads were pretty rough." All three would take turns in telling me something about those days in the plains.

When the A.F.B. was in full operation, they lost their 'sacred' hunting grounds. You might say that they were chased to another location, which they named as the Pines.

As time went on, they found new friends, with whom they hunted for many years. They were called the natives of this territory, who became expert guides for the deer hunt.

Fred brought up the time when their car was full of hunters, so much so, that he and Bob were riding in the trunk with the lid open. What they saw during this hectic ride was an experience that they have cherished all their lives. It was indeed a sight to behold! There on the side of the rugged road from which they all carefully observed, was a huge buck taking its afternoon siesta. Only the two that were in the trunk saw their quarry, and since the car was barely moving, they bolted out of there in seconds. Bob was the first to fire at this enormous beast. The car stopped and they all yelled, "Did you get 'um?" and Bob said, "You bet, and boy is he a dandy!" The fourteen pointer may have been their biggest buck in their years of hunting.

Their early living quarters was a log cabin with all outdoor facilities, something that most deer hunters of old can talk and laugh about. Some years later they stayed at Ed Howard's farm, a place of much comfort, warmth and good food.

Looking over some of Ben's literary work, he would say so remarkably well, "In the fall we'd see miracle greens, yellow and indescribable reds, leaves that fall from trees so tall, we" listen to the cold northerly breeze."

Many seasons went by when all three took home their prize bucks. During our interview, Bob took me upstairs and showed me the trophy room! Of course, they all took time to show me those cherished photos, too.

I asked them, "Have any of you ever been lost?" It took a while for Ben to tell me, "Oh, I guess I missed that certain trail back to camp!"

During those days at Sands, they saw a few coyotes, and managed to tag two black bears. Some years they had to trample through twenty-six inches of snow. Living in Marquette County during the month of November can sometimes be an awesome experience. And of course, one need not wonder why this part of Michigan is so cold and deluged with heavy snows, when his answer comes by looking at Lake Superior, the world's greatest fresh water lake.

The storytellers informed me that their stay at the farmhouse was most enjoyable, especially with Ed Howard's company. Sitting by the ol' wood stove listening to deer hunting stories is most satisfying. This is real camp talk!

I was rather curious to learn what is now in place of the A.F.B. since it was closed. The Sands bunch told me that it was converted into a manufacturing company.

I questioned them about what legacy they left for future generations. They agreed that all hunters be thoroughly educated in the field of hunting deer, such as gun safety, properly dressed, and being more aware of alcohol abuse. They are somewhat concerned about the lack of interest that young males have for the outdoors, such as hunting and fishing, especially in the wilderness, where one gains a real peace of mind, just tramping through pine plantations and hardwoods, or angling for some native speckle trout.

I really peppered these three with many questions, one of which was, "Did you ever come in contact with a Game Warden?" Their answer was quick, "You bet we did!"

I just remembered when Fred talked about Big Game hunting, he told me that he traveled in the Northwest territory, Alaska and Canada. Anyone that knows anything about this sort of hunting, Fred was in the right place. He saw what he was after and he conquered. Now I know why that polar bear license was so costly. Flying to Timbuktu, plus finding a guide and all that lodging was indeed an expensive exploration.

It was time now to end this very special interview. They made their last 550-mile voyage to a place they call, "The Plains of Sands". One would sense that they exhausted all avenues of adventure, but there was so much more they could have said about their half-century of pure enjoyment. It was also for these men of much wisdom and experience to pack their hunting gear and encase their guns and call it a grande finale. "From our hunting blinds time has made a change in muscle and mind, and we leave our foot prints on the Plains of Sands—Perhaps we will return again to reminisce, surely we would be welcomed by the open plains, the pines, the hills and those winding roads which have no end. Welcomed by the stately raven, as he sets atop a lonesome pine and calls out in eerie voice of warning which he sends—but surely there are written words in the sands of time, that we shall always be welcomed back home again to the plains of dear old Sands."

Fifty Years of Togetherness and Pure Satisfaction

THE LANGUAGE OF THE FOREST

Driving by a leafy residential area the other day, I noticed something that brought back a thousand memories, and this is what compelled me to write about the forest.

What I saw were two small tangling feet clearly visible from a huge pile of leaves. I thought for a moment that the owner of those feet was in some kind of trouble, but then I quickly pictured myself in the same heap and laughing like mad. I was hoping in a way that I would be next to jump in! While living in the Upper Peninsula during the autumn season, I had walked and driven for miles on tote roads that had been rarely touched by man. It was in these parts that I observed the wonders of nature. I was simply awed by the array of color, and had wished that what I saw, could have had the faculty of speech to tell the rest of the world about beauty at its optimum.

So here then is what you, the reader, will read and hear— the voices of your neighbors, the trees.

We show our presence annually, but especially during the early part of October. We are observed by the passerby and are admired by many, but we are ignored by some, and of course, we are slightly moved, to say the least.

True, we do boast of our variated colors, and rightly so, as we have been trying to show what our Creator can do. At first we are tinted with a shade of yellow, but in a few days we are at the pinnacle of the autumn season. We are not alone, mind you, in giving you this spectacular, as we are terribly proud to present our relatives and friends and also their relatives. So you see, we love company. We live and dine in forests, in groves, really most everywhere. Some of us are graduates, others undergraduates, but we still brush with amateurs and novices. We all share one goal, that being to fill the earth with glory and splendor.

With our colleagues we have weathered the four seasons, through wind, snow, rain and heat. In winter we survive the seemingly endless scourge of heavy snows and sub-zero temperatures. The advent of spring brings new life and vigor. The rays of the sun add warmth and a purpose. In the fall we are fully satisfied and become pompous, displaying a multitude of colors, and all this being for His honor and glory. We live for the people who have eyes to behold our majesty, and for the less fortunate to envision our just being there.

We're told that we possess something special, something extraordinary, something that man tries to imitate by hand and brush, but our veins are alive and fruitful. We supply man's planet with stupendous growth, some changeable, others not. Our chief purpose at this moment is to tell everyone that we are here to be observed, not to be loved, adored or worshiped, as this is contrary to our intent. One would really be a fool not to be impressed by our conspicuous appearance. It has occurred to us that there are moments when we cannot please the entire populace, either because of our immaturity or inaccessibility.

Once we have accomplished our mission, we become dormant and our leaves plunge to earth, providing laughter and fun for the youth, and enjoyment for those that just bustle in our midst. Before all this came to be, we provided shady nooks for picnickers. We were a forest covering a vast land, over knolls, ridges and cliffs, even swamps of twisted cedars. Now our leaves are as countless as the stars that measure up the sky. No one will ever know our count.

On so many occasions we have been hit relentlessly and buffeted by gales, and twisted and demolished by some of nature's vicious onslaughts. We fall aimlessly like distant kites. Somehow we find a resting place, some of us on the floor of the forest, while others among hedges, fence rows, precipitous cliffs, and places where man dare not.

We have been raked, stacked and piled, only to be destroyed by the hand of man. Even then we have given satisfaction to many by the smell of burning leaves, a tradition, I am sure, that has been carried on since the beginning of time. Rather strange that our scent should now be a merchandise.

We ride the lakes, the rivers, the rivulets, the streams and the creeks, and at times outlining the shores like garment fringes, often being caught and swallowed by little whirlpools. Logjams, too, have grabbed us from escape.

It is now the end of another season and another cycle for our being here. We venture to say that our brilliance never ceases, but we only rest for another beginning.

By the way, we have almost forgotten to tell you, that people in this part of the land, who have harvested small gardens, have come our way with their gunny sacks to fill them with our precious cargo. We were pleased to note that during all the winter months, we kept warm all their produce, which were their potatoes, carrots, beets, onions, cabbages, turnips and rutabagas.

The wonders of nature have fascinated me since I was a youngster tagging along behind my father, who was noticeably moved just by the mere smell of the forest, I would like to add to my narrative the following poems, which I wrote during my tenure in the classroom back in '72, and which have given me many pleasures of the forests:

A PINCH OF EVERGREEN

Famed a blazer of uncharted trail,
A boy set out one day in quest of untold beauty.
Gnats, mosquitoes slowed his pace,
With branch or fern he'd briskly, gently stroke his
    face.

Logs, stumps, and windfalls he'd encounter
Some he'd chop, others he'd hurdle.
The blade of his hatchet echoed beyond the trail
A smell of pitch and bark delighted his soul.

This knoll shrouded by hemlock, pine and balsam
Were his fondest greeneries.
A pause, and then another moment,
    just to pinch an evergreen
Offered added pleasantries.
Still another squeeze of balsam limb
Gave beauty of an inner world,
To just a boy, my son, Michael.

LANGUAGE OF THE FOREST

The forest is my domain,
I know, I've lived there all my life.
Browsing, watching, walking, leaping,
Listening, stomping, lying,
Vigilance is my trade.

Trees are my playground
Branches, boughs my look'n hideout
Charmed by this awesome sight
Just living there bewilders man of old.

97

Trees abound in countless number,
Each in its own turf, each on its own might.
Evil there is not, evil cannot be.
How do I know? Ask, for they speak with majesty.

Our language, it seems, is phenomenal
Like so many tongues of fire
Sounds and revelations by spruce
Towering hemlocks side by side
Befriended by sturdy ash
Protected by mighty oaks
Maples sending invitations
An array of colorful birch
Day's end serenaded by whispering pines.

'Tis true I am sought for game and trophy,
So are those who neighbor me,
Furred, feathered, and watered,
Our tongues permeate the darkest forest,
And man still wanders and wonders why this be.

Winter's Tree Stand

What Better Way to Meditate?

A Vast and Beautiful Panorama of Our
Forest's Timber

A MAN AMONG MEN

This is a story about a highly distinguished man, who just recently walked in our midst, and who left a lasting impression on this side of our troubled world. He was chosen among men to represent a hierarchical principality. Since his elevation to the pontificate, he has confounded the minds of high-ranking officials, and moved the hearts of countless numbers. He has traveled almost to the ends of the earth, seeking peace, friendship, goodwill. He has raised his hand in blessing throngs, uplifted his arms to greet millions of well-wishers. He has shaken the hands of unbelievers, as well as those who do believe. He has had a compulsion to embrace and kiss children, the invalids, and the less fortunate. This man, the 263rd successor of St. Peter, has the rare distinction of having the ability to speak in many tongues.

What is it about this man that men wish to see, to know, to talk with and to touch? People have walked, have sailed, have flown and have ridden just to get a glimpse of this man of peace and love.

Television has brought this controversial figure into our living rooms and in all places of relaxation. In his recent southern tours we wondered how he could have withstood the late summer's heat. His physical stamina bewildered those who followed him. It was his disciplined mind and body that gave him the power to follow a rigorous schedule. This was an attribute that he acquired while fighting the forces of evil of the Nazis. We are now beginning to see a certain charisma about this church leader.

His arrival in America was indeed a glorious one. This

Vicar of Christ was graciously received by our president, Mr. Reagan. People have waited for this holy man for months. Maintenance men have worked in the late hours of the night to prepare the stage for his presence. This teacher, writer and outdoor figure stood tall wherever he walked. He is now better known as Pope John Paul II.

This humble man talked to men of simple faith, as well as those steeped in theological theories. He not only mingled with those who were callous in their beliefs, but also listened to those who have been reaching for some sound knowledge of philosophy.

This globetrotter has undertaken the weight of the world on his shoulders, closely resembling the weight of his master's cross. He is extremely concerned about how nations live, their daily sustenance, and that all civilization be fully aware of the importance and sacredness of Christianity.

During the pontiff's sojourn in the Motor City, I had the good fortune of seeing and hearing this prolific man. One could readily surmise why he would be considered a man among men. In the arena of the 20th century gladiators, the pope blessed some hundred thousand spectators, and during his homily he stressed the need for social justice, for we were in a city of economical strife.

It was time now for this man of prayer to leave the confines of Pontiac's Silverdome. Once again he blessed, kissed, caressed, as he proceeded with Michigan's Hierarchy. Holding the symbolic crosier in his left hand, he waved his last good-bye. The stadium's multitude responded with a tumultuous roar, "Viva Il Papa". He turned toward his flock for the last time, and said, "God bless America." When the last glimpse of his pontifical robes disappeared in the exit, there was a personal feeling of not ever seeing him again.

This was not the end of his North American visit, as he still had another mission to complete. Fort Simpson, an Indian Reservation located near Edmonton, Alberta, Canada, was

John Paul II's next and final stop. His mission here was to see and speak to a tribe of Indians whom he had on his itinerary on a previous occasion, but weather conditions hampered the plane's landing. During his shortened stay at this post, His Holiness prayed, said Mass and spoke from a teepee-like sanctuary to several hundred Indian souls. He also parleyed with the tribe's chiefs and administered his papal blessing to the rest of the faithful.

A stiff northern breeze gave all indication that the advent of another winter was in the making. Chimneys on the houses of this tiny nestled village were puffing smoke from stoves giving heat or preparing the next meal. It was time now for this man of God to end his ten-day excursion to the North American Continent. He was quickly ushered into one of Canada's Airlines, and in a matter of minutes the world's Good Shepherd disappeared in the Canadian sunset.

PETER FORSYTH DUFFTON

This is a tribute to a man who had touched and moved the hearts of countless men, women and children. He was an extraordinary man, because he performed extraordinary deeds. It was clearly and unmistakably seen that he was everyone's friend; he was not known to have an enemy. His serious smile, his nod, his looks were his indelible traits. His cigarette, then a puff, his pronounced chuckle, his ever so delightful conversation were only his and only ours to remember. A sports enthusiast he was not, as this was not what made him great, but he was still a giant.

Whoever knew this most colorful character called him "Pat", though his name in full was Peter Forsyth Duffton, a native of Scotland. He was known to be deeply rooted in religious truths. He was not a graduate of higher learning, but you would often see or hear him discuss some past or recent philosophical question. Socrates, the ancient Greek philosopher, would have enjoyed having him as his pupil, molding characters and building sound minds. This is why he was a giant among men.

Music was his forte, though nothing prolific, yet possessing simplicity in its truest form. The violin, the piano, the organ were his special tools. It was evident that such a man experienced little, if any boredom. His solemn, sedate and graceful form gave music its optimum in interpretation. His love of musical tones changed the moods of those in his presence. Even his whistle caught the ears of passersby.

Besides his gusto for music, you would often see him by a pool table with his cue, chalk and tobacco and favorite vintage, telling his opponent his next plan of "attack". This was just another satisfying, comforting and un-provoking moment in the life of this special person.

"Really, what kind of a man was this? You ask. Was he trained to be so gentle, so kind, so considerate, so friendly, and so incredibly understanding?" No, even with his human frailties, it was just his way and philosophy of life. So many good things have already been eulogized about "Pat". Charisma was his.

You recall the many times he waited on you, and you often brushed shoulders with him in the aisles of the local grocery store. When you came home, you would inevitable be asked, "See Pat?" Without hesitation, you smiled and said, "You bet." He would often ask about you and yours. It was in this way that he exemplified his love and concern for family life.

The tiny village of St. Ignace was stunned, when it learned that "Pat" became seriously ill. The town was silenced when it further learned that its giant succumbed to a dreadful disease. There were many gifts, cards, spiritual remembrances and phone calls, all conveying some special message of good cheer to those who stood by. For "Pat's" health it was not to be, but rather for us to go on living and remembering how great this man really was. He ran his race and performed it flawlessly. His immediate family saw him complete this course, so did one who administered the unction of peace. Those who saw "Pat" then relate that he had no fear of death, but that he watched and listened attentively to the last holy gesture and felt a closeness of his creator. Then took place perhaps the most stirring moment for all mortals to witness and learn about. This giant among men left one last tear for us to remember, that life will always remain a beautiful mystery. REQUIESCAT IN PACE.

THE CAREY MISSION

In the course of many years Niles has been blessed with good education, skilled engineering productivity and sound religious beliefs. Today we will bring to light some of the highlights of the early Baptist Ministry.

Recently I read Mike Cain's account of the Carey Mission. I would like to bring you closer to some of the happenings in this colony of worshipers.

I always did like the word Mission, as it has a clear dimension for adventure, expedition, hardship, and a special place where people gather to pray, to listen to the Word of God, to talk and enjoy each other's cooking.

For the people who travel the Niles-Buchanan Road, you will note a large boulder on the corner of Phillip and Niles-Buchanan roads on the right side going west. Mounted on this field boulder is a bronze plaque with the inscription, "Carey Mission founded in 1822 by Isaac McCoy. This tablet placed in 1922 by Fort St. Joseph Chapter D.A.R. (Daughters of American Revolution)."

Undoubtedly, it was at this very spot that the city of Niles first mushroomed. The Mission had marks of hard-working men and women, man helping man, all dedicated to the worship of their Creator.

When this Mission first started, there were indeed constant fears of Indian uprisings, but the people were resolute in making a place of worship. For this is why they came with horses and wagons, oxen and a few cattle. This was big bush country, there was much land to be cleared. Not too far from their landing was the Big River, the St. Joseph, surely a place for easy travel by the many Indian tribes that paddled their way on canoes. Along came the white man and fur traders who lured the red men with homemade brews and distilled liquors. With the advent of whiskey, came trouble, big trouble, as the early settlers were trying to befriend the Indians, and eventually evangelize them.

As you stand by that boulder bearing the name of Carey Mission, you picture yourself standing by some crude looking buildings, such as a school house, a chapel, barns, workshops, stables, a blacksmith shop and a grist mill propelled by oxen. Isaac McCoy was a Baptist Missionary whose ambition was to administer to the Potawatomis who lived along the Big Water, the River, and also near Lake Michigan. He did make friends with two French fur traders, and together they helped the Indians with the ways of God. Of course, living so primitively meant that the people were exposed to many diseases, sicknesses and early death. In due time, however, the white man did teach the Indian many things besides an understanding of God. They were taught to speak the English language, farming and how to take care of orchards and vineyards.

The Carey Mission was named after William Carey, the first Baptist Missionary to arrive in Indiana in 1794.

Some of the dignitaries that participated in honoring the Carey Mission in October 1922 were Rev. Henry T. Scherer, and Mr. Tom Hance, the mayor, who devoted much of his time in making Niles a productive city. Other clergymen included Rev. C. L. Barnes and Rev. Alfred Trennery. Since this was an occasion of worthy note, there were many from Indiana who came to make this a memorable event. Some Indians, too, were part of this celebration.

A book entitled, "Wolves Against the Moon" by Julia Altrocci, will give us a more vivid picture of the white man's struggle with the Indians and life on this early Mission. This piece of writing can be found in the Niles Public Library. They say that the Carey Mission lasted about ten years, and then moved to the State of Kansas.

The complete story of the Carey Mission comprised a much more detailed account that what your present writer has recorded. From this short narrative we can assume that the early Baptist Church left its rich mark on the populace of Niles.

It must be noted that among McCoy's closest associates was Joseph Bertrand, a French-Indian by birth. A story has it that he helped McCoy's people by supplying them with much needed food at the Mission. The Indians considered the area around Bertrand's Trading Post as Buffalo Country. It could very well be that Bertrand provided the church colony with buffalo meat and treated hides for warmth.

YESTERDAY'S YOUTH

If you've been feelin' kind of blue lately, maybe I can help to put a smile on your face. My story today will be all about you, when you were a little girl, whether you were a tomboy or just a plain petite and demure person. And you, sir, when you were just a kid, poor, rich or whatever, perhaps the leader of the pack, or one just being led. At any rate, I wish to talk about you, about all of us. Some of us are city slickers, just plain townspeople, or maybe you lived in the country, and I hope that you are not ashamed to tell our readers that you were raised on a farm.

It is so true that we all had a fling with some youthful activity or recreation. In my following thoughts I am going to picture you in some situation in that place you called home.

If you came from the farm, we're watching you as you walked behind your father tending the plow being driven by his sturdy team of Belgian horses. One of your more pleasurable chores was going to the chicken coop to fetch some fresh eggs. You were so careful not to bother the hen, but it was just her nature to give you a peck on the hand. After the chores you had some frisky moments in the front yard, running and chasing your brother or sister until you were all tuckered out. Those of you who had baby chicks sheltered behind the kitchen stove, watched your father or mother chopping up hard boiled eggs to feed the little ones.

It was a warm summer day when you and the gang sat on a fence chewing at a blade of grass, wondering what to do next, or you could have been just thinkin'.

I'm sure you have fond memories of running through some

tall grass, much of it was over grown buttercups that waved in the summer breeze. You were once told about the ol' fable that if anyone placed a buttercup under you chin and it showed yellow, you liked butter!

You also remember the ol' swing in your yard, the first one would always be a tire that your father tied to a big limb of a tree. Then a bit later he made the real kind, when a bunch of you kids tried to reach some low flying clouds. How about all the water pumps and buckets you'd see. Did you ever wonder why so many of today's greeting cards picture old barns and houses, pumps and buckets, barbed wire fences, old churches and schools? I'm sure that you recall your son or daughter, and your grandchildren saying to you, "Gee, it sure must have been nice back then!"

How many times have you looked at those musty books and photos, just lookin' and reminiscin'. I'll bet there must have been some heartbreakers in that pile. Just rummaging through all your stuff kind of touched your heart, didn't it?

The day that your daughter or grandchild picked you a bouquet of wild flowers, sneaked in the house somehow, and said to you, "Here." Don't you wish that were yesterday? And even if you were a man, and your own kin handed you a dandelion, wouldn't that be a tug at your heartstrings?

I saw a little boy clumsily wading through a puddle of rain water the other day, and if that didn't ring a bell, as it took me back a few scores, when my mother scolded me for getting my shoes wet!

How many of our youthful games have changed in the course of time? Hide-and-go-seek is still around. How about hop scotch, jacks and marbles? I am sure there are many others, even some that you made up yourself and handed down to the next generation and all their kids.

March winds brought you and all your friends out with your kites, and sending signals up the string with cardboard disks. Can you remember making all these contraptions?

Aren't you glad that your father taught you how to saw and chop wood for the winter months ahead? He taught you how to use a sawhorse with a buck-saw or crosscut. Those of you who have never seen this operation, then you really haven't lived.

Of course, there was always someone that was special to you, someone with whom you exchanged glances. It was not that important, but still it was a beautiful encounter.

All those days you spent throwing, skimming and batting rocks into a big pond, and maybe this is why you became so fond of baseball.

Halloween was something special in your neighborhood. All of you used to go masquerading during your trick or treat runs. It was different than today, as you didn't appear to be too demanding.

Your visits with your grandparents were moments that will live forever. Sunday came along and everybody went to church, and you never asked why?

I kind of think that your school days were rather special, too. You never had to worry about catching a bus, and you very rarely complained about walking all that distance.

Then came Christmas and you'd always go to that certain spot to chop down that fir tree. Can you remember the times that you were in Christmas plays at the school, singing carols and riding in horse drawn sleighs?

I sincerely hope that this little piece of writing will bring back some beautiful memories of the good ol' days.